Following God

First Steps
for the NEW CHRISTIAN

STARTING AND FINISHING THE RACE WITH STYLE

for the NEW CHRISTIAN

STARTING AND FINISHING THE RACE WITH STYLE

EDDIE RASNAKE

AMG Publishers

Following God

FIRST STEPS FOR THE NEW CHRISTIAN

Sixth Printing, 2008

ISBN: 0-89957-311-8

Cover and text design by Phillip Rodgers
Editing and layout by Rick Steele
Cover illustration by Florence Anderson

Printed in Canada
12 11 10 –T– 10 9 8 7

This book is dedicated to the late

Danny Hall

Danny was my roommate in college and my
best friend in high school. We were diamonds in
the rough and new Christians together. His days
on earth were too short, but he is remembered.
I guess his mansion got finished before mine.

Acknowledgments

This work has been a labor of love for me. It has taken me back to those early days as a new Christian and has made me appreciate those who helped me take my first steps in the Christian life. I would like to thank those who have helped me to learn these truths, and those who have enabled me to share them with you. Special thanks to Dan Penwell for the idea, to Rick Steele for the great job in editing, to Dale Anderson, Trevor Overcash, Warren Baker, Phillip Rodgers and the whole gang at AMG Publishers for being commited to the Word of God and for doing so much to help people study it for themselves. Most of all, I remain grateful to the Lord Jesus, who continues to teach me step-by-step what it means to follow Him with a whole heart.

EDDIE RASNAKE

About the Author

Eddie Rasnake met Christ in 1976 as a freshman in college. He graduated with honors from East Tennessee State University in 1980. He and his wife, Michele, served for nearly seven years on the staff of Campus Crusade for Christ. Their first assignment was the University of Virginia, and while there they also started a Campus Crusade ministry at James Madison University. Eddie then served four years as campus director of the Campus Crusade ministry at the University of Tennessee. In 1989, Eddie left Campus Crusade to join Wayne Barber at Woodland Park Baptist Church as the Associate Pastor of Discipleship and Training. He has been ministering in Eastern Europe in the role of equipping local believers for more than a decade and has published materials in Albanian, German, Greek, Italian, Romanian, and Russian. Eddie serves on the boards of directors of the Center for Christian Leadership in Tirana, Albania, and the Bible Training Center in Eleuthera, Bahamas. He also serves as chaplain for the Chattanooga Lookouts (Cincinnati Reds AA affiliate) baseball team. Eddie and his wife Michele live in Chattanooga, Tennessee with their four children.

About the Following God Series

Three authors and fellow ministers, Wayne Barber, Eddie Rasnake, and Rick Shepherd, teamed up in 1998 to write a character-based Bible study for AMG Publishers. Their collaboration developed into the title, *Life Principles from the Old Testament*. Since 1998 these same authors and AMG Publishers have produced five more character-based studies—each consisting of twelve lessons geared around a five-day study of a particular Bible personality. More studies of this type are in the works. Two unique titles were added to the series in 2001: *Life Principles for Worship from the Tabernacle* and *Living God's Will*. These titles became the first Following God™ studies to be published in a topically-based format (rather than character-based). However, the interactive study format that readers have come to love remains constant with each new Following God™ release. As new titles are being planned, our focus remains the same: to provide excellent Bible study materials that point people to God's Word in ways that allow them to apply truths to their own lives. More information on this groundbreaking series can be found on the following web pages:

www.followingGod.com

www.amgpublishers.com

Preface

The Christian life is an exciting journey! You may just be getting started or just starting over. Wherever this book finds you, I want you to know that every step you take toward the Lord is worth it. The Bible calls the Christian life a "walk"—that means that it is made up of a lot of little steps in the same direction. It is not a leap or a sprint. I hope this study will help you start out on the right foot and stay there.

One of the reasons I felt this book needed to be written was that I know how important those first steps are in the Christian life. Because I came to Christ as an adult, I can remember more clearly the struggles and questions I had, the answers that were most meaningful, and the needs of those early days. I have tried to faithfully put down on paper the most important things for beginning the Christian walk. What I have found over the years is that many people who have been Christians for a long time still struggle in some areas of their walk because they were never really grounded in the basics of the faith. The things we study in this book are the things you will never outgrow in walking with God. These are the principles you will live out until the Lord returns or calls you home.

I have written this Bible study with the goal of self-discovery. I have tried to make the Word of God the authority instead of the author. It is my aim that you would often experience the joy of looking to the Bible and hearing God speak from its pages. I have also written this study to point you to application. "Knowledge makes arrogant" but application (or trying to apply) makes us humble. None of us has arrived. We are all on the same journey as pilgrims. What I have learned from my own successes and failures has been poured into this project.

After twenty-five years as a Christian, I have not arrived yet. I take comfort in knowing that the apostle Paul said basically the same thing when he wrote Philippians 3 after twenty-five years as a Christian. I am not all that I ought to be, but by God's grace I am not what I used to be, and my hope is that I am not yet what I am going to be. I am on this journey of the Christian life with you—**Following God.**

Following Him,

EDDIE RASNAKE

Table of Contents

Your Position 1

Growth 15

Abiding 31

Dealing With Sin 43

Bible Study 57

Personal Devotions 71

Prayer 85

Producing Fruit 99

Faith 113

Hope 125

Love 139

Stewardship 155

How to Follow God 169

New Testament
Reading Schedule 173

step one

Your Position

"What has happened to you?" The question is as fresh to me today as it was my freshman year in college when I first became a Christian. With the question, Danny, my best friend from high school, acknowledged that my life had become different. Like many today, I had grown up in a broken home—fractured by my father's alcoholism. My teen years were spent wandering without a father's example and guidance. Instead I followed the crowd into marijuana and drugs. By the time I was a senior in high school, I was not only using them, but also selling them. I was the biggest dealer in school. Spiritually, I was lost. I called myself an atheist, but I was not an honest one. It wasn't that I had studied and wrestled and concluded there could be no God; it was just that I didn't care. I thought the purpose of life was to have as much fun as you could have before you died. Yet with all the adventures and experiences I pursued, fulfillment remained elusive. It still seemed just inches from my grasp. The "highs" I lived for were just mini-vacations from the emptiness I battled. When someone very close to me was arrested and sentenced to prison for selling drugs, it was as if blinders fell off my eyes. I was rudely confronted with the reality that my life was going nowhere. The only difference between him and me was that he got caught.

What has happened to you?

About this time, the Lord brought a friend into my life that patiently and honestly shared with me what it means to be a Christian. Mack was a fellow I worked with, and at first I wasn't interested in his faith, but as I got to know him, I saw in his life the things I wished were true of mine—peace, joy, love, and contentment. After several months of watching his life, I decided I wanted what he had. With his help, near the end of my first term of college, I asked Christ to come into my life one night at work. It wasn't a huge emotional experience. Charlton Heston didn't come into the room and part the couch we were sitting on. Angel harps didn't begin playing. But I remember a pervading sense of peace and rightness. A few days before, I had been walking across campus to a biology exam and encountered Gideons handing out New Testaments. I took one as a joke, and told the fellow I was walking with that I needed as much help on the test as I could get. That little Bible lay, forgotten, in my backpack until I came home from work that night, a new creation in Christ. I immediately began reading in Matthew's Gospel, and for the first time, the Bible made sense. I encountered Jesus on every page.

I hadn't set about trying to reform my life, but when Danny asked, "What has happened to you?" I realized my life was changed, different. Within a few short weeks he joined me in the faith. Though he is in heaven now, I have thought a lot about Danny's question. I suppose I am still answering it today. You see, though I knew my life was different, and I knew what I had done, I didn't fully realize all that God did. I am still learning more about all that took place when I first trusted Christ. That which seemed to me a simple choice, set in motion a complex working of God in my life. In this week's lesson, we want to look at all that changes when we meet Christ.

WE ARE ACCEPTED

One of my favorite times of the day is sunrise. It is a beautiful thing to be out in God's creation and to begin with total darkness and to gradually see the growing light until the sun peeps over the horizon. Each morning, God, the master artist, lays out the skies as His canvas and covers it with beautiful colors, welcoming the coming day. For individuals who place their faith in Christ, salvation is as a new day dawning. Our present reality is different than it was before. As we seek to understand more fully this new day that is dawning in our lives, we want to see it as God sees it—from His perspective. That perspective is found in His Word, the Bible.

In this lesson, and the ones to follow, we will look at many different passages of Scripture. For some of you this will be something you are already comfortable with. For others, you may not be used to studying the Bible. If you are in that camp, let me offer some practical advice from my own experience. When I became a Christian as a freshman in college, I didn't know Philippians from Philistines. As I would sit in church, the speaker would say, "Turn to..." and give a Bible verse to look up. Everyone around me seemed to go right to it immediately. It wasn't so easy for me, though. Often, I would still be looking for that verse when the speaker and the audience had already gone somewhere else. Very quickly though, I learned two helpful things: First, my favorite page in the Bible became the one titled "Table of Contents." At the front of your Bible you should find a similar page that will tell you where to find the different books of the Bible. Second, some Bibles are made with thumb indexes to help you locate the different books more easily. If yours doesn't have those, you can purchase tabs at your local Christian bookstore that you can stick in yourself to do the job. From time to time you may hear preachers or others call your attention to references such as 2 Corinthians 5:17. You might even see references like these in Bible study or devotional material. Don't be intimidated! The first number is the chapter (5), and the numerals following the colon are the verse number (17). Actually, the verse division system was added into the Bible after it was written to make it easier for folks like you and me to find a particular passage. (Aren't you glad?)

📖 Read through 2 Corinthians 5:17. What does it say about the one who is "in Christ"?

_____

_____

_____

_____

_____

> *"Therefore if any man is in Christ, he is a new creature; the old things passed away; behold, new things have come."*
>
> *2 Corinthians 5:17*

To be "in Christ" means we have placed our faith in Him and invited Him into our hearts. If we have genuinely done this, then a new day is dawning. We are a new "creature" or "creation" as most Bibles translate it. That is a powerful term, since man can manufacture (make something out of something else), but only God can create (make something entirely new). This verse tells us that for such a person, old things have passed away and new things have come. This doesn't mean that a new Christian is instantly perfect—other verses make it clear that we need to grow as Christians—but it does mean a new day has dawned. My present experience is different than my past.

📖 Look up these verses and write down what you learn there about what is different in your life since meeting Christ.

John 1:12

_____

_____

John 15:15

_____

_____

Romans 5:1

_____

_____

_____

These verses share some exciting truths! If I have "received" Christ (welcomed Him into my life). John 1:12 tells me, then I have been given the right

Word Study
JUSTIFIED

The word, "justified" means to be declared righteous or just by the penalty for unrighteousness being paid. It refers to our being made righteous in a judicial sense. Our sins have offended Holy God and created a debt which must be paid. We cannot pay that debt ourselves, but through faith in Christ, we can be "justified" by the payment of His death for our sins. An easy way to remember what it means is through this little saying: "justified = just as if I'd never sinned."

Word Study
GRACE

The word "grace" (*charis*) in the Greek language (the language in which the New Testament was originally written) has the same root word as "gift," and the two words are very similar. The common definition for grace (unmerited favor) is accurate, but the idea is incomplete. God's grace to us is undeserved favor when, in fact, we deserve His wrath.

Your Position **DAY TWO**

to become a child of God. God doesn't take me in as a servant, but as part of His family! John 15:15 reveals that Jesus doesn't consider us slaves, but rather, His friends. Romans 5:1 adds that we have been "justified," and we now have peace with God. Once we were His enemies, but now we are His friends, and even part of the family!

From time to time, we are going to see "religious" terms pop up that you may not be familiar with using since they aren't part of every-day conversation. When we encounter such terms, this study will define them either in the text or in the column to the side of your page (as with "justified" here). Hopefully you'll find this helpful.

One of the richest books in the Bible that tells us all that is true of us now that we are Christians is the book Paul wrote to the Ephesians. We'll be spending a good bit of time there in this lesson. We want to finish today's homework with a brief look there.

📖 Look at Ephesians 1:6. What does it say about us?

_____

_____

_____

_____

_____

_____

God has freely bestowed grace on us through Christ, who is called *"the Beloved."* The King James Version of the Bible translates the phrase as *"He hath made us accepted in the beloved."* I like that word "accepted." Because God loves His Son, Jesus, He is acceptable to Him. If I am in Christ, then I get to be accepted in Him. Even though I used to be an enemy of God, through Christ I am now His friend. That is my present reality. I am "accepted in the Beloved." In Matthew 3, when John baptizes Christ, verse 17 records the words God spoke from heaven. The literal rendering is "this is my son, the Beloved, in whom I am well pleased."

WE ARE ADOPTED

Several years ago, I was part of a celebration at our local airport. Dozens of Christians gathered there to welcome home a family in our church who was returning from Bulgaria with a three-year-old little girl they were adopting. Excitement was in the air as we saw the plane taxi to the gate. Cheers erupted as the happy parents walked into the terminal with this precious girl, Molly, in their arms. She wasn't sure what to make of us, but warmed up when I said, "Hello" to her in her native tongue. As I led our group in prayer, we thanked God for her and prayed for the new life she would have in this loving Christian family. For her, the whole world had changed. Her first three years of life were spent in an institutional orphanage with dozens of children for each worker to care for. Suddenly she had two adoring parents all to herself. She went from the impoverished country of Bulgaria to the abundance of America. She went from the meager resources of that orphanage to the plentiful provision of this family. We couldn't help but rejoice with her. Yet at three years old, she probably didn't understand right away how her whole life was going to be different. Did you know that you and I have been adopted out of a bankrupt world to live in a new country with our heavenly Father, who has limitless resources? We'll look at that truth today.

📖 Read Ephesians 1:1–3 and then answer the questions that follow.

How does Paul identify the Christians at Ephesus (verse 1)?

_____

_____

_____

What does he wish them (verse 2)?

_____

_____

_____

What does he say they have in Christ (verse 3)?

_____

_____

_____

Did you see what Paul called those Ephesians? He called them **saints!** I used to think the title "saint' was reserved only for people like the disciples or Joan of Arc. But as I studied the Bible, I found that it uses the term to refer to anyone who is a Christian. You may not think of yourself as a saint, but God sees you that way. In order for us to be accepted, we have to be "in" the Beloved. That position means that when God looks at us, He sees Jesus. In Ephesians 1:2, Paul wishes the Ephesian "saints" grace and peace. This was a common greeting among Christians back then, and basically he reminds the Ephesian church about what God has given them. Perhaps most impacting in these verses is what he says in verse three that they have in Christ. Paul says that they have been blessed with *"every spiritual blessing in the heavenly places in Christ."* In other words, everything that heaven has to offer, we have in Christ.

Some people live their whole lives trying to get things from Christ, yet the truth is that we already have *"all things"* in Christ. When we got Him, we got everything else that there is to get. Theologians call this reality "positional truth"—or things that are true of us because of the position we hold. When a person becomes president of the United States, with that position come the keys to the White House and access to Air Force One. He can stay in a hotel if he wants. He can buy an airline ticket to travel if he so desires. But why would he? His position gives him a free place to live and a free means of travel wherever he needs to go. It comes with the office. Positional truths are those things that "come with the office" of being a Christian. Paul says when we became Christians, God blessed us with every spiritual blessing there is in the heavenly places in Christ. The verses that follow in Ephesians chapter 1 are a partial catalog of those blessings.

Did You Know?

? WHO ARE THE SAINTS?

The Roman Catholic Church has throughout its history recognized certain individuals as official saints. It "canonizes" them for extraordinary deeds of charity and faith, and gives them public recognition. But on November 1st, commonly called "All Saints Day," the Roman Catholic Church also recognizes every believer as an unofficial saint. In Ephesians 1:1, Paul instructs us that even if we don't feel like we deserve such a title, God sees each believer as a saint.

📖 Look at Ephesians 1:4–5. What is the spiritual blessing of verse 4, and when did it happen?

_____

_____

_____

_____

_____

The blessing here is that God chose (selected) us *"before the foundation of the world"* (meaning "before the foundation of the world was laid" or "before creation"). The creation occurred "in the beginning" of time, but not in the beginning of God. Time is not an eternal commodity since it began with the creation and will end after the millenium. Yet God chose us before time even was invented. It is important to read all of the verse. It says that God chose us "that we should be holy and blameless before Him." God's intent is that salvation be much more than simply "fire insurance" (protecting us from the fires of hell). He desires us to be holy and blameless and has guaranteed that we will be that way in heaven since that is the only way we can have a relationship with Him.

Identify the blessing of Ephesians 1:5 and what you think it means.

_____

_____

_____

_____

_____

One of the many blessings we have in Christ is that we have been *"predestined"* to adoption as sons. Through Jesus Christ, we have been adopted into God's family as children. God's predestination accomplishes this blessing. Predestination as a biblical word basically means "to guarantee." In this case, it doesn't refer to salvation but to adoption. In other words, God has guaranteed that all who are saved will be adopted into His family as sons. We are adopted, as verse 5 tells us, *"according to the kind intention of His will."* God could have chosen to save us as slaves instead of as sons. We are His children purely by His grace (verse 6). First John 3:1 celebrates this truth saying, *"See how great a love the Father has bestowed upon us, that we should be called children of God."*

DAY THREE

WE ARE ATONED FOR

We've been looking at the many things that are true of us because we are in Christ. In the process, we've found that many of these truths have technical terms in religious and theological circles. They may seem a little intimidating at first, but once we understand what they mean, they become something precious to us. One such term is "atonement." In the Old Testament times, one day a year was observed as

Yom Kippur ("the day of Atonement"). Every year, sacrifices were made for the sins of the people—to atone for them for a time. Yet each year, the sacrifices had to be made again. But when Jesus came and gave His life for us, His perfect sacrifice atoned for our sins—for all time. There is no need for any more sacrifices.

📖 Read Ephesians 1:7–8.

What blessing do you see here for us?

_____

_____

_____

Practically speaking, what do these blessings mean to you?

_____

_____

_____

The blessing here is redemption, and means "to release on payment of a ransom." The word draws on the cultural practice of slavery in ancient Jewish life. When people were unable to pay their debts, they were sold into slavery to work them off. They could be redeemed or bought back by a family member or friend who would pay the debt. This is what Christ has done for us. We had a debt we could not pay because of our sins. Because of His love and grace, He paid a debt He did not owe.

Looking at verses 7–8, answer a few more questions.

What was the payment for our "redemption" (see the first part of verse 7)?

_____

_____

_____

What does this tell you about its cost to Christ?

_____

_____

_____

Why do we receive the blessing mentioned in these verses (see the end of verse 7)?

_____

_____

_____

Doctrine
ADOPTION

In the culture of ancient Rome, adoption was a significant relationship. Once adoption had taken place, not only was the adopted child granted the rights of a natural-born child, but the relationship was also irrevocable. One could disown a natural-born child, but not an adopted one. When Paul uses this term to describe our salvation, he pictures a secure relationship.

The ransom for us could not have been paid monetarily, since *"the wages of sin is death"* (Romans 6:23). Christ purchased our redemption with His blood, which indicates the giving of life. This was not just any life either, but "God, made flesh," worth far more than any human. The only reason we have received this blessing is the riches of God's grace, which according to verse 8, God has "lavished" upon us. The word "grace" is repeated three times in these first few verses and is showcased as the sole basis for *"every spiritual blessing"* (verse 3) in which God has blessed us.

📖 Take a look at verses 8–10.

What is the blessing mentioned here?

_____

_____

_____

Doctrine
ATONEMENT

An easy way to remember what the word "atonement" means is to break it down like this: **atone = "at one."** In other words, atonement, the act of covering over or canceling sin, brings two who are divided back together. Our sins separated us from God, but Jesus' sacrifice "atoned" and made us "at one."

God, according to His good pleasure, has revealed to us *"the mystery of His will"*—the summing up of all things, both in heaven and on earth, in Christ. We have been made privy to the plan of God for the ages. Colossians 2:2–3 and Romans 16:25 teach us God's mystery is that He (God) is revealed in a human form (Christ), and thus all wisdom and knowledge are revealed through Him to the world. As 1 Corinthians 1:30 puts it, *"By His doing you are in Christ Jesus, who became to us wisdom from God. . . ."* This mystery is a blessing to us, as 1 Peter 1:10–12 tells us that the mystery of Christ was both the expectation of the prophets and the longing of the angels; yet we have the privilege of both seeing it and experiencing it. What a glorious time in which to live!

Your Position   **DAY FOUR**

WE ARE ANTICIPATING

When one considers the blessings that are already ours because we are Christians, it seems almost too good to be true. We are *"accepted in the Beloved"* (Ephesians 1:6). The One who knows us best loves us most! We have been adopted into God's family and have been redeemed by the payment of His own life. All our sins have been forgiven; grace has been lavished upon us; and the mysteries of God's will have been revealed. Truly, we have been blessed with every spiritual blessing heaven has to offer in Christ. And yet, the most amazing thing is, **the best is yet to come!** In 1 Corinthians 2:9, Paul tells us that, *"Eye has not seen and ear has not heard,"* nor has it *"entered the heart of man, all that God has prepared for those who love Him."*

📖 Identify the blessing in Ephesians 1:11–12 and what that means from your perspective.

_____

_____

_____

_____

The blessing mentioned in these verses is the inheritance of God. There are two equally valid ways of reading this verse. The New American Standard Bible translates it, *"We have obtained an inheritance,"* pointing to us as receiving the blessings of God. An equally legitimate translation could be "We are made an inheritance" reflecting us as God's inheritance which Christ bought back. It is unclear which is meant here, but both are true, and the concepts seem to be linked in verse 14 (see also Deuteronomy 32:9). We have an inheritance in Christ, but we also are an inheritance which Christ has purchased.

📖 Read Ephesians 1:13 and answer the questions below.

What is the blessing mentioned in this verse?

_____

_____

_____

How do we get this blessing?

_____

_____

_____

_____

_____

The blessing mentioned here is that we have been "sealed" in Him with the Holy Spirit of promise. At salvation, God's Spirit came into our hearts to live as a promise of that which is to come. In order to receive this blessing we had to **a)** listen to the true message, and **b)** believe that message (or place our trust in the Savior that message declared). It is interesting to think about what this verse essentially says. When God's Spirit comes into our hearts, He "seals" us or secures us in Christ. Believers receive the Holy Spirit at the point of salvation. This is the time when the "baptism by the Holy Spirit" that Scripture speaks of occurs. Being *"filled with the Spirit"* as Paul speaks of in Ephesians 5:18 is not getting more of the Spirit, but yielding every area of our lives to the Spirit's empowering and direction: having our lives filled with God's Spirit as opposed to self.

📖 Looking at Ephesians 1:14, identify the blessing mentioned in that verse.

_____

_____

_____

_____

The blessing here is that we were given the Holy Spirit as a "pledge" or a down payment. In modern Greece, this same word for "pledge" is used for what we call an engagement ring. It literally means earnest money or a down payment—something given beforehand to confirm what is promised. This same Greek word is used figuratively of the Holy Spirit, which God the Father has given to believers in this present life to assure them of their future inheritance in eternity. It is the promise that God will come for His *"possession,"* the Church, also figuratively called His bride in other Scriptures (Revelation 21:2, 9).

Word Study
SEALED

The Greek word translated "sealed" here speaks of the kind of seal placed on official documents where an imprint was placed in melted wax. Often there were two seals connected by a thread. If the thread was unbroken, it was proof that the document had not been opened and altered since it was written. This same Greek word was used of the Roman seal placed on Jesus' tomb. To break that seal without authorization was punishable by death. It was a mark of guarantee, backed by the full authority of the one who placed it.

FOR ME TO FOLLOW GOD

I hope you are beginning to grasp some sense of how blessed we are to be Christians! To quote an old preacher from the hills of Tennessee, "If that don't light your fire, your wood's wet!" Although all these blessings happened the moment we met Christ, we must grow into understanding them fully. As you can see, most of what we looked at this week came out of the first chapter of Ephesians. Later in that same chapter, Paul writes his prayer for the Ephesian believers: *"I pray that the eyes of your heart may be enlightened, so that you may know what is the hope of His calling, what are the riches of the glory of His inheritance in the saints, and what is the surpassing greatness of His power toward us who believe"* (Ephesians 1:18–19). These truths, as awesome as they are, cannot be grasped at once. God must first enlighten us, so that this information moves from our heads to our hearts. A key step in that enlightening process is taking the time to think through how these truths apply to our lives. At the end of each lesson, we will spend some time in application, helping you to live out the truths you are learning. I hope you will find this helpful.

 As you consider the blessings we have looked at this week, which ones did you already understand, and which ones were new concepts for you?

	Already Understood	New Concept
Accepted in Christ	☐	☐
Adopted into God's Family	☐	☐
Redeemed from Slavery to Sin	☐	☐
Forgiven of All Our Sins	☐	☐
Lavished with Grace	☐	☐
Revealed the Mystery of God's Will	☐	☐
Given an Inheritance	☐	☐
Sealed by the Spirit	☐	☐
Given the Spirit as a Pledge	☐	☐

For those issues that were new to you, it may be helpful to talk with your pastor or a trusted Christian friend to make sure you understand all that is meant by them. If a wealthy relative had died and left you items in his will, understanding what those items were would be a priority. In the same way, understanding all that is already ours in Christ ought to be very important to us.

> *"I pray that the eyes of your heart may be enlightened, so that you may know what is the hope of His calling, what are the riches of the glory of His inheritance in the saints, and what is the surpassing greatness of His power toward us who believe."*
>
> *Ephesians 1:18–19*

Take a look again at Ephesians 1:3. How does the verse instruct us to respond to the blessings God has given us?

_____

_____

_____

_____

God, who has so richly blessed us, Himself deserves to be blessed (to adore and thank for all benefits) by us. Perhaps the most important place to start in applying this week's lesson is to take some time to thank God for these many blessings. Take a few minutes to go through each of the blessings we looked at as they are listed below, and thank the Lord in prayer for them. You may want to use the space provided as a place to write down this prayer.

Accepted in Christ

_____

_____

_____

Adopted into God's Family

_____

_____

_____

Redeemed from Slavery to Sin

_____

_____

_____

Forgiven of All our Sins

_____

_____

_____

Lavished with Grace

_____

_____

_____

Revealed the Mystery of God's Will

_____

_____

_____

Given an Inheritance

_____

_____

_____

Sealed by the Spirit

_____

_____

_____

Given the Spirit as a Pledge

_____

_____

_____

 One final application to think about: All that we have studied in this lesson are the blessings that belong to believers. They are of no help to you if you are not a Christian. If you have any reason to question whether or not you really are a Christian, take some time to read through the appendix at the end of this workbook called "How to Follow God." If you aren't sure you are a Christian, then this will help you make sure.

Remember, we are not Christians simply because we go to church or because we read the Bible or because our parents raised us to be Christians. Ephesians 1:13 indicates that to be a Christian we must listen "to the message of truth" and also believe. We will look more fully at what it means to believe in the lesson on faith, but suffice it to say, it is more than simple intellectual belief. It is active trust, and it involves our will.

Notes

Notes

step two

Spiritual Growth

When the Bible speaks of beginning a relationship with God, it uses interesting terminology. It refers to this event as a "spiritual birth." Jesus told Nicodemas in John 3 that he needed to be *"born again."* Of course, Nicodemas was understandably confused. As Jesus went on, He explained that one must be born of the flesh and of the Spirit. Think about the picture Jesus paints here. He equates beginning a relationship with God with childbirth. The obvious point that leaps out at us once we understand the analogy is that "getting saved" is only the beginning of that relationship. We understand right away that birth is only the beginning of physical life. We have experienced this, and we see it all around us. Yet the same is true of spiritual life—birth is only the beginning. From that point we enter a process of growth.

The Christian life is not an arrival, but a pursuit. We are in the process of becoming what the Lord wants us to be, but we haven't arrived there yet. Paul makes an amazing statement in Romans 13:11, when He says, *"For now salvation is nearer to us than when we believed."* Though our eternal security is insured the moment we become God's children, in a sense, our salvation is a gradual process that is not perfected until we are given perfect bodies in

The Christian life is not an arrival, but a pursuit. We are in the process of becoming what the Lord wants us to be.

eternity. The Scriptures lay out that process in three key components. We were saved from the penalty of sin when we first believed—that component is called "justification." We are in the process of being saved from the power of sin—that process is called "sanctification." We will one day be delivered from the very presence of sin—that point is called "glorification." We haven't gotten there yet, but we will.

GROWTH IS A PART OF LIFE

Think of how many things around us grow. Trees, flowers, and animals grow. Even people grow. Everywhere we look, we see examples of the growth principle. Yet, often in our minds we limit it to the most basic rudiments. We think of growth only in the realm of the physical. Yet that is not an accurate portrayal of what is going on around us. For example, just because we are full-grown physically, doesn't mean we are fully developed socially. I know many adults who have never grown up. Hopefully, we do not stop growing and developing mentally just because we stopped growing physically. Clearly, growth and development are not limited to the physical realm. This lesson begins by looking to the Lord Jesus and learning from His own example about this issue of growth.

📖 Read Luke 2:52 and write down each of the areas in which Jesus developed and how you think that relates to us.

_____

_____

_____

_____

It really is an amazing thought to realize that Jesus had to grow up! Even though He was God in the flesh, He still had to grow and develop. Nowhere in Scripture do we find a clearer portrait of the reality of progressive development. Jesus "kept increasing" in each of these areas. Perhaps the most important truth to glean from this verse though is the ways in which He grew. He continued to develop in wisdom, stature, favor with God, and favor with men.

Look at Luke 2:52 again and write out what you think regarding these four areas of development.

Jesus kept increasing in wisdom—

_____

_____

Jesus kept increasing in stature—

_____

_____

_____

Word Study
KEPT
INCREASING

The word translated "increased" in Luke 2:52 ([KJV]; translated "kept increasing" in the NASB) is in the imperfect tense in the Greek. This particular tense is used only in statements describing facts of events that happened in the past but that unfolded in a continuous or linear manner. In other words, they did not happen all at once. It not only tells us that the action happened, but also how it was happening. Jesus "kept increasing" in each of these areas.

Jesus kept increasing in favor with God—

_____

_____

_____

Jesus kept increasing in favor with men—

_____

_____

_____

_____

That Jesus *"kept increasing in wisdom"* is an incredible thought that makes no sense unless we understand it to refer to Him in His humanity. As God, Jesus had no need to learn anything, but as man, He identified with us in our need to grow intellectually. He studied and learned things, just like you and I do. In the same way, each of these areas clearly refer to the humanity of Jesus. He kept increasing in stature which speaks of His growing and developing physically. He kept increasing in favor with God—He grew and developed spiritually. And He also grew and developed socially, continually building relationships with others.

What a powerful thing it is to understand that Jesus, while on earth, experienced physical and spiritual growth in much the same fashion that you and I have experienced it. But as God, He did not make the mistakes you and I make. Therefore, His life is an example worth following.

SPIRITUAL GROWTH IS A PROCESS, NOT A POINT

Spiritual Growth   DAY TWO

If we are to understand spiritual growth, we must first grasp one key concept: spiritual growth is not a point, but a process. It is an area where we are to continually progress. We need to have a testimony of a point when we placed our faith in Christ, but if that is the only testimony we have, something is wrong. The Lord ought to be doing something in our lives in the present, not simply in the past. One of the ways the Bible talks about spiritual life is calling it a "walk." Colossians 2:6 says, *"As you therefore have received Christ Jesus the Lord, so walk in Him."* Think about that idea. The Christian life is a "walk." It is not one giant leap, but a lot of little steps in the same direction. Comprehending the idea of spiritual growth as a process greatly helps us. Just like newborn babes, new Christians are going to crawl before they walk. They won't start out eating T-bone steaks or digesting complicated theological doctrines. Sometimes the church is better at feeding the spiritually mature than those who are newly growing. Hopefully, you will find that this study doesn't make that same mistake.

📖 Look at the verses that follow and write what you learn about this idea of spiritual growth.

The Christian life is a "walk." It is not one giant leap, but a lot of little steps in the same direction.

Mark 4:28

_____

_____

_____

Philippians 3:8–14

_____

_____

_____

> **"Not that I have already obtained it, or have already become perfect, but I press on in order that I may lay hold of that for which also I was laid hold of by Christ Jesus."**
>
> **—the apostle Paul after 25 or 30 years as a Christian**

In each of these passages, we see that growth is a process, not a point. In Mark, a clear analogy is given from nature: when a plant grows, it begins with the blade, then the head, then the mature grain. As Miles Stanford puts it in his classic book, _Principles of Spiritual Growth_ (Lincoln, NE: Back to the Bible, 1997, p. 12.) "For most of us it has been a long season of growth from the tiny green blade up to the 'full corn in the ear.' So many seek to settle for this stage: saved, with heaven assured—plus a pacifying measure of Christian respectability, at least in church circles." Clearly, that view of faith sees salvation as nothing more than "fire insurance"—saved from the fires of hell. But God desires to do more than rescue us from the penalty of sin. He wants to make us like Him, and He is patiently working toward that goal. Paul captured it well when he wrote, _"Not that I have already obtained it, or have already become perfect, but I press on in order that I may lay hold of that for which also I was laid hold of by Christ Jesus."_ The amazing thing is that Paul had been a Christian for twenty-five or thirty years when he wrote that!

📖 Compare 2 Peter 1:3–4 with 2 Peter 3:18 and write what you learn.

_____

_____

_____

_____

_____

The message of 2 Peter 1 is a powerful one: everything we need for life and godliness is found in knowing Christ, but we must **grow** in knowing Christ. It is not a point we are looking for, but a process of growth. The results of such a knowledge are significant—not only can we partake of His nature, but we also can escape the corrupting lusts of this world. Peter begins his second epistle with this message, and then closes with the clarifying idea that we _"grow in the grace and knowledge of our Lord."_ It is not a point we are looking for, but a process of growth.

Dr. A. H. Strong once gave the illustration of a student who asked the president of his school whether he could not take a shorter course than the one prescribed. "Oh, yes" the president replied, "but then it depends upon what you want to be. When God wants to make an oak, He takes a hundred years, but when He wants to make a squash, He takes six months." Strong goes on to point out that "growth is not a uniform thing in the tree or in the Christian. In some single months there is more growth than in all the year besides. During the rest of the year, however, there is solidification, without which the green timber would be useless. The period of rapid growth, when woody fiber is actually deposited between the bark and the trunk, occupies but four to six weeks in May, June and July" (Miles J. Stanford, *Principles of Spiritual Growth,* Lincoln, NE: Back to the Bible, 1997, p. 12.) There is no shortcut to spiritual maturity. We attain this maturity when a spiritual truth becomes a part of our character.

SPIRITUAL GROWTH HAS AN ASSURED OUTCOME

W hen we say that growth is a process instead of a point, that does not mean that the outcome is uncertain. God is committed to our spiritual growth, and He has guaranteed that it will one day culminate. A newborn baby doesn't have to strive to grow longer legs or a bigger body. The genetic blueprint is in place, guaranteeing that the body will grow. All that is needed is the proper food and exercise. We need to trust the fact that God is working in our lives. He isn't finished with us just because our sins are forgiven. In fact, that is only the beginning. He wants to mature us – to grow us up into who He wants us to be. In today's lesson we want to focus on the goal God has for our spiritual growth—what He is working toward. The bottom line is this: He wants us to be like Christ. He wants to work in our lives so that we are more like Him.

📖 Look at Philippians 1:6 and summarize the message you find there.

_____

_____

_____

_____

_____

In Philippians 1:6, Paul makes a definitive statement with two key points: **1)** it is God who began the good work in you, and **2)** He **will** complete the work He began. When Paul says he is confident of this, the Greek word he used for "confident" is in the perfect tense, indicating a settled, certain conclusion. As you look at your salvation, you may be able to identify decisions and choices you made, but you must realize that God is the one who brought the gospel to you and you to Himself. It is the work of the Spirit of God to convince us of our need for Him. This becomes a freeing truth when we realize that God began it and that He is committed to finishing the job He started.

📖 Read Romans 8:28–30.

What is the "good" God is working toward in verse 28 according to verse 29?

_____

_____

_____

> *"For I am confident of this very thing, that He who began a good work in you will perfect it until the day of Christ Jesus."*
>
> **Philippians 1:6**

How certain is the outcome of verse 29?

_____

_____

_____

How does God view the process of our growth according to verse 30?

_____

_____

_____

_____

The promise of Romans 8:28, one of the greatest in Scripture, is that God causes everything in our lives to be working for our good. The good spoken of is not the good of ease and comfort, but of being conformed to the image of Christ. God has "predestined" or guaranteed that the work He began in us will be completed. The outcome is not in doubt. In fact, if you look at verse 30, you will notice that it is worded in the past tense. God already sees His work as finished. Time is nothing to God. He can see all the way to the end of time, and He has already seen to it that the job of our becoming like Christ will be finished one day. Even now, He is causing everything that happens in our lives to work toward that good purpose.

📖 Look at Genesis 1:26–27. What was God's original purpose in creating mankind?

_____

_____

_____

📖 How was the fulfillment of this purpose changed after sin entered the picture (see Genesis 5:1–3)?

_____

_____

_____

_____

God originally created man to reflect His image, but through sin that image has been distorted so that He can no longer be clearly seen in us. We see in Genesis 5:3 that after the fall, when Adam and Eve have children, these children do not reflect the image of God, but the image of fallen Adam. It is sort of like a gelatin mold that gets dented. After the damage is done, everything else that comes out of the mold reflects those dents. In the same way, we carry the dents of sin passed on to us by our forefathers. What God is doing in our salvation is re-creating in us that image of Christ. It is not a one-time event but a process—a process He will keep perfecting until the "Day of Christ Jesus" or the day Jesus comes back for us.

Second Corinthians 3:18 tells us, _"But we all, with unveiled face beholding as in a mirror the glory of the Lord, are being transformed into the same image from_

God is in the process of re-creating His image in us, and that is a step-by-step process.

glory to glory. . . ." That last phrase literally reads in the original language, "out of glory into glory" or in other words, from one glory to the next. Bit by bit God is in the process of making us into what He wants us to be. We needn't get impatient with how long it takes, for He is working from and for eternity.

SPIRITUAL GROWTH HAS A MEASURABLE OBJECTIVE

When a builder starts to build a house, before he digs the foundation or nails the first board, he first must have a set of plans—a clear picture of what the finished product is to look like. He refers back to those plans again and again throughout the construction process to measure his progress and to make sure he stays on track. Our spiritual lives ought to be like that. We want to be disciples, yet for many of us, we really don't know what direction we should be seeking. Because we don't have a clear understanding of what God's plan looks like, we don't really know which direction we should be heading, and we don't have any way of knowing if we are making progress. But it doesn't have to be that way. The Scriptures do offer a clear plan of what it means to be a disciple of Jesus. Today, we want to look at these Scriptures so we can be sure we are making progress.

📖 Looking at John 15:7–8, identify each of the characteristics listed here that "prove" one is a disciple and then write what you think each characteristic means in the space provided.

One who "abides" in Christ

_____

_____

_____

_____

One who has the Word abiding in him

_____

_____

_____

_____

One who prays and sees those prayers answered

_____

_____

_____

_____

BEING A DISCIPLE

"and so prove to be My disciples…"
(John 15:8)

Here are some very practical things that prove to all that we are followers (disciples) of Jesus:

- ✓ We abide in Him
- ✓ His words abide in us
- ✓ We ask from Him, and He answers
- ✓ We glorify Him
- ✓ We bear His fruit

One who glorifies God

_____

_____

_____

_____

One who bears fruit

_____

_____

_____

_____

These verses identify five characteristics of a disciple:

1) A disciple is one who **abides** in Christ, consistently walking with Him; A disciple is not perfect, but is constantly in pursuit of perfection. To abide has the idea of "staying connected." The context is that of a branch staying connected to the vine as its source of nourishment and energy. When we are in fellowship with Jesus, His life flows through us.

2) The **Words of Christ** abide in him. Colossians 3:16 says, "_Let the word of Christ richly dwell within you. . . ._" For a disciple, the Word is his authority and also his delight. The truths of Scripture should constantly nourish us.

3) His life is characterized by **prayer** and **answers.** This characteristic of prayer is built on the foundation of the first two and implies a lifestyle of communion and communication with God. This speaks not of the activity of prayer alone, but of genuine prayer—his spirit connects with the Spirit of God.

4) He **glorifies God** (as opposed to self). When a disciple abides in Christ and the words of Christ fill his life—when his life is characterized by answered prayer and fruit-bearing—he brings glory to God.

5) He **bears fruit.** Fruit is the logical consequence of the other characteristics. Remember, these verses are in the context of Christ's parable of the vine and the branches. The ultimate evidence that we are abiding in the vine is through our bearing fruit.

Fruit is always the evidence of maturity. It is the final proof of the nature of a plant. When you see apples growing on a tree, you know that it is an apple tree. The same is true of Christians. As we mature spiritually, the fruit of our new nature begins to be seen.

Take a few minutes to reflect back on John 15:7-8. What significance do you see in the progression?

_____

_____

_____

_____

_____

_____

> When we are in fellowship with Jesus, His life flows through us.

_____

_____

_____

_____

This passage is incredibly significant in helping us to know what it means to be a disciple of Jesus. As we consider these verses, the order is important. The foundation of discipleship is abiding in Christ. If you think about it, what this says is that your relationship with God is the most important thing – not your study or service. Those flow out of a healthy relationship with God. If we start anywhere in the list but with abiding, we will err. Our Christian life will not have the balance God desires. If we start with Bible study, we will focus on information instead of transformation and we will become proud because of how much we know instead of how we live. If we start with prayer, it will become a religious activity instead of a relationship. If we start with ministry (fruit-bearing) we will focus on working for God instead of walking with God. There is nothing wrong with Bible study, prayer and service, but they must be built on the foundation of abiding in Christ.

APPLY So how does a Christian know if he is becoming a disciple? Jesus gives the definition of a disciple in John 15:7–8. He says that if we bear fruit, we prove to be His disciples. We must ask ourselves the following questions:

Am I abiding in Christ?

_____

_____

_____

_____

Do I know how to let the Word abide in me, and am I choosing to do that?

_____

_____

_____

_____

Is my walk producing a prayer life that is effective?

_____

_____

_____

_____

"Does my life bring glory to God?"

_____

_____

_____

_____

"Is there fruit?"

_____

_____

_____

_____

_____

FOR ME TO FOLLOW GOD

Avoid making the mistake of not knowing what the goal of your Christian life should be or how you should attain it. Be brave enough to look at your own life and ministry. Ask yourself, "Am I a disciple according to John 15:7–8?" As we close out this week's study, we want to seek to apply what we have learned to our own lives. We have been looking at the principle of growth, and application of truth is a key to seeing growth happen. It doesn't matter how much we know intellectually if that knowledge doesn't change how we live.

If we aren't careful, it is easy to get discouraged when the newness of our Christian life begins to wear off, and we realize that although some things have changed right away, other things haven't changed as quickly. We may compare ourselves to other Christians and feel unworthy because we aren't as far along as they are in some area. Or worse, we may become proud because we think we are further along than they. Yet everyone progresses spiritually at a different rate. What God changes right away in one person, He may set aside to work on later in another.

Bill Bright, founder of Campus Crusade for Christ, used to speak of two fraternity roommates who trusted Christ in the early days of his ministry. They were stereotypical fraternity men, reminiscent of John Belushi in the movie _Animal House._ Both were overweight and loved to drink beer. Both made genuine commitments to Christ, and very quickly Dr. Bright could see changes in their lives. But those changes were not uniform. One was convicted by the Lord that he should stop drinking beer. The other sensed a need to exercise and lose weight. Soon these changes began to produce conflict in their relationship. They became judgmental of each other and used their own progress in one area to criticize the other's lack of progress in that area. It took time for them to realize that God was working in both their lives, but in different ways.

As we look to our own growth, we may be discouraged when we see how far we need to go; nevertheless, we should be able to take courage in seeing how far we have already come. And we should find hope in realizing that God isn't finished with us yet. We are not all we ought to be, but we are not all we used to be either; and by God's grace, we are not all we are going to be.

 Look at Luke 2:52 again and evaluate how you think you are doing in each of these four areas of personal development.

Increasing in Wisdom—

Little progress   ⬅   1   2   3   4   5   ➡   Good progress

Increasing in Stature—

Little progress   ⬅   1   2   3   4   5   ➡   Good progress

Increasing in Favor with God—

Little progress   ⬅   1   2   3   4   5   ➡   Good progress

Increasing in Favor with Men—

Little progress   ⬅   1   2   3   4   5   ➡   Good progress

We are not all we ought to be, but we are not all we used to be either, and by God's grace, we are not all we are going to be.

As you look at these four areas of personal development: the intellectual, the physical, the spiritual, and the social, think through what would be some good short-term goals to aim at to make progress in each of these areas. Be careful not to set unrealistic goals that are sure to fail, yet, at the same time, you need to aim at something. If you aim at nothing you are sure to hit it!

FOR THE NEXT THREE MONTHS

Intellectual Goals:

_____

_____

_____

_____

_____

Physical Goals:

_____

_____

_____

_____

_____

Spiritual Goals:

_____

_____

_____

_____

_____

Social Goals:

_____

_____

_____

_____

APPLY One of the goals God has for us is to produce His fruit in us. Take a minute to look through the list of the "fruit of the Spirit" (Galatians 5:22–23). Consider how you are progressing at seeing these things manifested in your character. Obviously none of us are perfect, but our aim ought to be predictability—that these characteristics or fruit become what people normally see in us. In fact, you could almost call these nine character traits the "ultimate New Year's resolution" list.

Love

_____

_____

_____

Joy

_____

_____

_____

Peace

_____

_____

_____

Patience

_____

_____

_____

Kindness

_____

_____

_____

If you aim at nothing you are sure to hit it!

Goodness

_____

_____

_____

_____

Faithfulness

_____

_____

_____

_____

Gentleness

_____

_____

_____

_____

Self-Control

_____

_____

_____

_____

APPLY Underline the one or two main areas in which you have already begun to see growth as God develops your character. Place a check-mark next to one or two areas in which you most want to see progress.

- ❑ **Love**
- ❑ **Joy**
- ❑ **Peace**
- ❑ **Patience**
- ❑ **Kindness**
- ❑ **Goodness**
- ❑ **Faithfulness**
- ❑ **Gentleness**
- ❑ **Self-Control**

It is important that you recognize that these are the qualities God produces in us, not the things we must produce for Him. We cannot grit our teeth and make these a reality by simply trying harder. If we could, we wouldn't need a Savior. What we can do though is to begin to desire the things God desires for us. And we can pray for Him to work in our lives in these areas.

As we close out this week's lesson, write out a prayer asking God to produce in you His character in those areas in which you know growth is lacking. That very awareness is evidence of God's work in you, for Philippians 2:13 says, *"For it is God who is at work in you, both to will and to work for His good pleasure."* Even the desire for growth is evidence of His work in our lives!

_____

_____

_____

_____

_____

_____

_____

_____

_____

_____

_____

_____

_____

_____

_____

_____

_____

_____

_____

Notes

Notes

Abiding

Picture in your mind a cold, juicy, luscious bowl of grapes. The grapes are plump and full, with little beads of moisture condensing on their surface. Your mouth waters as you imagine the explosion of flavor as you bite down on one. I don't know about you, but I love grapes. I'm getting hungry just thinking about them! In John chapter 15, Jesus makes an important point about grapes. He says that you and I as believers are like the branches of a grape vine. God wants to produce through us something far more attractive and desirable than those grapes. He wants to produce in us His life. He made us for this very purpose. But for this objective to be realized, it takes more than simply being a branch—it takes abiding.

One of the methods of Jesus in teaching us the truths of spiritual life is to take something we understand and use it to teach us something we do not understand. We often call this kind of instruction analogy, or allegory, or most commonly, a parable. In the previous lesson, we looked at John 15:7–8 and saw what it takes to prove one is a disciple. We saw that a disciple is one who abides or remains in Christ; His words abide in such a person; a disciple asks and receives and brings glory to God and bears much fruit. These verses in John 15 are found in the middle of "the parable of the vine," and since they are the clearest picture

"I am the vine, and you are the branches"
—Jesus

of what it means to be a disciple of Jesus, we will look more closely at each of the components of being a disciple in the next few lessons of this study. This week we want to begin answering the question, "What does it mean to 'abide' in Him?"

Abiding **DAY ONE**

THE PARABLE OF THE VINE

In John 15, Jesus gives a parable to explain how we are to relate to God. In this parable, He took something that the people of His day understood clearly and used it to educate them about something they didn't really understand. Theirs was an agricultural society. Even if they were not farmers, they would be familiar with the agriculture of their area. Everyone had seen vines of grapes and had eaten from them. Jesus used this simple picture from nature to help the people of His day understand how to relate to God.

📖 Read through John 15:1–17.

Who are the main characters in this parable?

_____

_____

_____

What is the main application from the parable of the vine?

_____

_____

_____

_____

What results when we "abide" in Him?

_____

_____

_____

The prophet Isaiah wrote, "A vineyard of wine, sing of it! I, the LORD, am its keeper; I water it every moment lest anyone damage it, I guard it night and day" (Isaiah 27:2–3).

Jesus' parable of the vine has three main characters: God the Father, who fills the role of the "vinedresser" or gardener; Jesus, who is the vine; and believers, who are the branches connected to the vine. The main point of the parable is that it is our staying connected to Christ that produces fruit, just as the branch's connection to the vine produces grapes. A branch doesn't make grapes—it merely carries them. The grapes are produced on the branch by the life of the vine flowing through it. God desires for His life to flow through us so that He can bear His fruit through us. As we saw in the previous lesson, God wants to produce in us the fruit of Christian character (love, joy, peace, patience, kindness, goodness, gentleness, faithfulness, self-control) and the fruit of Christian ministry (evangelism, discipleship, acts of charity and service).

As you think of this analogy of the vine, it is important to understand that in a parable Jesus makes one main point. Here that point is "abide in Me and you will bear fruit." Even though a parable is very useful in helping us to understand something, every parable breaks down eventually. Not everything that is true of a vine and its branches is true of Christ and His believers. What is true is that like a vine and its branches, we must stay in close connection to Him if He is to bear fruit through us.

We see that abiding is so important to the Christian life, but how do we do it practically? What does it mean day-to-day to abide?

📖 Look at John 15:9. What do you learn there about what it means to abide?

_____

_____

_____

_____

Jesus calls us to "abide" in His love. Abiding is really all about preserving a relationship. We must keep our relationship with Christ healthy if His life is to flow through us. Think about what this verse is saying. Jesus loves us. The Greek word for "love" in John 15:9 is used to describe Christ's unconditional love for us. He is totally committed to us. What He desires is that we stay in that realm of love. At this point the analogy of the vine and the branches begins to break down, for the vine does what it does because of the laws of nature. It has no love relationship with the branch. We cannot look at Christ as if He were only the supply depot for our needs. He loves us intimately and desires fellowship, not just service.

The love of God is more than mere sentiment—it is empowerment. It is God's very life flowing through the vine of Christ into us. We dare not miss a drop of what He offers us, for it is this life that produces in us His character, and His works.

> **Abiding is really all about relationship. We must keep our relationship with Christ healthy if His life is to flow through us.**

ABIDING MEANS OBEYING

Abiding **DAY TWO**

An important distinction to make in understanding what it means to abide is the difference between "relationship" and "fellowship." Think about your earthly family. You have a relationship with your earthly mother and father that is unchangeable. They gave birth to you. Nothing can ever change the fact that they are your biological mother and father. The relationship cannot be changed, but the fellowship can. Let's say you do something terrible and your parents are so upset that they kick you out of the house and disown you. All fellowship with them would cease, but that would not change your relationship to them. They will always be your biological parents. In the same way, once we are born into the family of God, we have an unchangeable relationship. He is, and always will be, our heavenly Father. But choices we make do have an effect on our ability to enjoy the benefits of that relationship—our fellowship with God. This distinction is at the core of what it means to "abide" in Him—abiding is all about staying in fellowship with Christ.

A picture God has given us of our relationship with Him is our earthly family. God wants to relate with us as a father to his children. As our heavenly parent, He is committed to us with an unchangeable love. But our choices can get in the way of our experiencing His love.

One of the ways an abiding relationship expresses itself is in obedience. In fact, in this passage of John 15, Jesus links obedience as a tangible expression of our love for Him. If we love Him, we will obey. This doesn't mean that we earn His love by our obedience, but rather that obedience is the proper expression of gratitude for His love. Because God loves us and seeks our best, He will discipline us if our lives are marked by rebellion and constant disobedience. He does this not to punish us, but to instruct us and protect us from the consequences of a disobedient life. What we need to realize is that God is the one who gives us the ability and the power to obey. If we rebel and try to live independently of Him, we won't have access to His empowering strength to bear the fruit of obedience.

📖 Read John 15:10 again. What does it teach us about the role of obedience in abiding?

_____

_____

_____

What do you think obedience means practically in a relationship with God?

_____

_____

_____

Think of your relationship to God as that of a child to a father. We cannot hope to have a good relationship with our earthly fathers if we consistently disregard the things they say are important and the things they instruct us to do. A good earthly father doesn't desire to control the lives of his children as a dictator over them, but he does desire to guide and instruct them in the right way. Yet the father/child relationship will be affected negatively if a child refuses this loving fatherly instruction. In fact, children will rob themselves of a father's help if they refuse his instruction. This seems to be the point Jesus is making about abiding. If we walk in relationship with God, He will be guiding us and instructing us and even empowering us, just as the life-giving sap flows from the vine into the branches. If we are continually disobedient, we will choke off the flow from the vine and it will be impossible to bear fruit. Jesus said it well in Luke 6:46, *"Why do you call Me 'Lord, Lord,' and do not do what I say?"*

As you look at your relationship with God and evaluate the benefits of abiding and obedience, you may be asking, "Does it all depend on me?" If you think about it, if we can obey in our own strength, why do we need a savior? If we can be good for God on our own, why do we need His help?

📖 Look at John 15:5. What does Jesus say we can do on our own without Him?

_____

_____

Jesus makes it clear that apart from Him we can do nothing in this arena of bearing fruit. We can't even make raisins, let alone grapes. Our obedience is not something that earns a relationship with God, but something that flows out of it. But if we are walking in fellowship with Him, we will respond in obedience to what He instructs and initiates in our lives.

📖 Consider what Jesus says in John 14:15.

What does Christ say will result if we love Him?

_____

_____

_____

How does John 14:16–17 relate to this?

_____

_____

_____

Jesus says if we love Him, we will keep His commandments. He goes on in verses 16–17 to explain how we do that: *"and I will ask the Father, and He will give you another Helper . . . that is the Spirit."* The word "and" makes it clear that this is not a separate point but a continuing of the first point. It is all-important that, as we look at the applications God calls us to in His word, we recognize that we will only be able to accomplish those as we draw on the power of His Spirit indwelling us. Otherwise, we will find ourselves trying to obey God through self-effort, and we will ultimately fail. We see this necessity even in Christ. As John 14:10 puts it, *". . . the Father abiding in Me does His works."*

BEING FILLED WITH THE SPIRIT

Abiding DAY THREE

Another way the Bible speaks of this "abiding life" that we are looking at in John 15 is the idea of being "filled" with the Holy Spirit. You can see how one idea builds on the other. Abiding in the Vine (Jesus) is all about having the life of the vine flowing out to the branch. Being "filled" with the Spirit is all about the same thing. We want to be *"filled up to all the fullness of God"* (Ephesians 3:19). We don't want just a drop of God in us to add a little color. We want to be full of Him. Christian writer Watchman Nee wrote a book entitled *The Release of the Spirit* in which he stated that while God's Spirit lives within every believer, He has often not been allowed access to every part of that believer's life. What is needed is for the indwelling Spirit of God to be released into every area of our lives. In today's study we want to consider how this happens.

📖 Take a look at Ephesians 5:18.

What does it say we are not to do?

_____

_____

> **Our obedience is not something that earns a relationship with God, but something that flows out of it.**

What does it say we are to do?

_____

_____

In Ephesians 5:18, the apostle Paul commands us *"Do not get drunk with wine . . . but be filled with the Spirit."* What interesting terminology Paul uses here! If you look at the phrase *"be filled with the Spirit,"* at a glance it may appear that we are like empty cups waiting to have the Spirit of God poured into us. That is not an accurate understanding though. If you look at the book of Acts, you find that the phrase, "filled with the Spirit," is applied to the same group of people on a number of different occasions. In other words, it isn't something that only happens once. In fact, this phrase in the original Greek is in the present tense. A fair, alternative translation would be "be being filled with the Spirit" or "be continually full of the Spirit."

📖 Now look at Ephesians 5:18 again. In this verse being filled with the Spirit is contrasted with being drunk with wine.

What similarities are there between being Spirit-filled and being drunk?

_____

_____

_____

_____

_____

What differences are there?

_____

_____

_____

_____

We often speak of someone who is drunk as being "under the influence" of alcohol. In that sense, the idea has common ground with being filled with the Spirit. In both cases the person is under the influence of an outside agent. In both cases that influence results in altered behavior. The two are vastly different though, because being drunk with wine produces many negative behaviors, while being filled with the Spirit of God produces His character and life in us.

📖 Take a look at Ephesians 5:19–21. What are some of the results mentioned here of being filled with the Spirit?

_____

_____

_____

The verses that follow Ephesians 5:18 mention four specific results are evident in people who are filled with the Spirit of God. **First,** they speak to one another with psalms, hymns, and spiritual songs. In other words, they become a spiritual encouragement to others. **Next,** they are singing and making melody with their hearts to the Lord, displaying contagious joy.

They have a song in their hearts. **Thirdly,** spirit-filled people are continually giving thanks for all things. They become grateful—they appreciate the ways their lives have been blessed. **Finally,** they become "subject" to one another. In other words, they begin to be concerned about others instead of thinking only of self.

Those who are abiding in the vine will begin to bear the sweet grapes of God in their lives and character. They are the kind of people each of us likes to be around and the kind of people God wants us to emulate as He works in our lives.

THE IMPEDIMENTS TO ABIDING

Jesus commands us, *"Abide in me, and I in you"* (John 15:4). He does not suggest this, He commands it. This means that we should do it, but it also assumes there is the possibility we won't. Abiding is not about whether or not we are Christians, nor whether or not we will have a relationship with God. Our level of abiding indicates whether or not we will walk in fellowship with God. To understand fully the principle of abiding, we must understand what can keep us from it. Imagine the pipes that channel water into your house and through it. If you turn a faucet on and no water comes out, you don't automatically assume that terrorists have bombed the local water plant. No, you understand that there is likely some problem on your end. You have a clogged pipe somewhere. The life of God is always flowing toward the believer, but there are things a believer can do (or not do) that can clog the flow of that life. Today we want to consider from Scripture what some of those clogs can be.

📖 Read Ephesians 4:30.

What potential danger is identified in this verse?

_____

_____

Looking at verses 29 and 31, what causes do you see suggested for "grieving" the Holy Spirit?

_____

_____

_____

_____

Word Study
"ABIDE IN ME"

The New Testament was originally written in the Greek language. The statement in John 15:4, *"Abide in Me"* is in the imperative mood in the original Greek, which means it is a command, not a suggestion. It is also in the "active voice" indicating it is something we must do, not something which is done to us.

One negative thing we can do to hinder our fellowship with God is to "grieve" His Spirit who lives within us. The sins identified in verses 29 and 31 point to specific things we can do that offend God. These "sins of commission" are actions we do that violate God's commands and will. They may include breaking one of the ten commandments or some action that runs counter to God's revealed will elsewhere in Scripture. It grieves the heart of God when we are disobedient, and maintaining our fellowship with Him requires that we deal with such sins His way. A closely related idea is found in Hebrews 10:29 where it speaks of insulting the Spirit. The root word used here has the idea, "to treat injuriously, to reproach." It is a stronger word than to "grieve" the Spirit. When a believer *"go[es] on sinning willfully after receiving the knowledge of the truth"* (v. 26), he is reproaching and insulting the Spirit of grace.

📖 Look at 1 Thessalonians 5:19.

What potential danger is identified in this verse?

_____

_____

_____

Looking at verses 16–18 and 20, what causes do you see suggested for "quenching" the Holy Spirit?

_____

_____

_____

📖 *Doctrine*

OUR RELATIONSHIP WITH THE SPIRIT

- We can grieve the Spirit (Ephesians 4:30)
- We can quench the Spirit (1 Thessalonians 5:19)
- We can resist the Spirit (Acts 7:51)

Another negative thing we can do to hinder our fellowship with God is to "quench" His Spirit who lives within us. The sins identified in the verses before and after verse 19 seem to point not so much to specific things we do that offend God as much as things we don't do. These are "sins of omission," failing to do something God has commanded, willed or led. The Holy Spirit is compared in Scripture to fire. When we fail to obey His leading in our lives, we throw water on the fire of God in our lives and bring His work in and through us to a halt. This action may include failing to share our faith as He has commanded, not giving to His work as He leads us to, neglecting some act of kindness, or failing to be of service in some other way. Quenching God's Spirit breaks fellowship with Him just as much as sins of commission, though we tend to view sins of commission more seriously. Both are distasteful to God, and both must be dealt with in His way.

📖 Take a look at Acts 7:51.

What potential danger is identified in this verse?

_____

_____

_____

What causes do you see suggested for "resisting" the Holy Spirit?

_____

_____

_____

_____

To whom is this verse addressed?

_____

_____

Another negative thing we can do to hinder our fellowship with God is to "resist" His Spirit Who lives within us. The sins identified in the context around this verse seem to point not so much to isolated acts as much as a pattern or lifestyle of not being open to God. One who resists the Spirit is one who, because of spiritual blindness, works against God instead of for Him and doesn't even realize it. We see that it is the Pharisees and religious leaders of Jesus' day that are addressed here, and they are identified as *"stiff-necked"* (stubborn) and *"uncircumcised in heart and ears"* (insensitive to God). Resisting the Spirit involves a lack of surrender to Christ's leading because of rebellion or ignorance (not recognizing what God is doing). Blindness to the work of God naturally results when we allow unconfessed sin to remain in our hearts. Resisting the Spirit could be called a "sin of submission," not submitting to God's authority and control.

A car with a clogged fuel injector will sputter and stall. It will not run properly or smoothly. A pipe with a clog in it will not permit water to run through it as it should. A person whose arteries are clogged with cholesterol will inevitably suffer a heart attack. In the same way, Christians who grieve, quench, or resist the Spirit will discover that the flowing of God in and through them has been hindered. Each of these passages we have looked at in Day Four of this study speaks of how we relate to the Spirit of God. If we are truly Christians, the Spirit of God has come into our hearts to live. We have been sealed by the Spirit into Christ (Ephesians 1:13). He has been given to us as a pledge from God, a promise that God will complete the work He began in us (Ephesians 1:14). Being filled with the Spirit does not mean we get more of the Spirit, but that He gets more of us. Another way of looking at it is that although the Spirit is **resident** in the life of every Christian, He is not always **president** of that life. We need to live lives under the influence of God. That is what He desires for us.

FOR ME TO FOLLOW GOD

Abiding  DAY FIVE

God desires to fill us with His Spirit so that His life is continually flowing through us. Just as a branch connected to the vine bears the fruit of that vine, a Christian who abides in Christ will bear the fruit of Christ. We saw in John 15:7–8 that the first step to proving we are His disciples is that we abide in Him. We want to finish this lesson by looking at what we need to do to apply this principle of abiding to our lives.

APPLY What is the main thing you learned about your relationship with God from looking at the vine and the branches?

_____

_____

_____

_____

_____

_____

_____

As we looked this week at the difference between a "relationship" with God and "fellowship" with God, that distinction may have been a new concept for you. It is important to be able to separate these two in our minds. Look at the statements below and match each item on the right to one of the items on the left.

Our relationship with God is…

Our fellowship with God is…

- changeable
- unchangeable
- maintained partly by us
- eternally secure
- maintained by God

As we consider our fellowship with God, we know that obedience is related to abiding. We need to be willing to do what God says and not do what He says we shouldn't do. But we rest in the knowledge that He will help us to keep His commands. He gives us the power to do what He asks us to do. In fact, He lives within us. By His Spirit, He has taken up residence in our hearts. We have a relationship with Him through His Son, and fellowship with Him through His Spirit. We saw from Scripture that there are three sins that adversely affect our fellowship with God, and these three sins are woven into how we relate to His Spirit in us. We grieve Him when we do what He says not to do. These are the **sins of commission.** We quench Him when we don't do what He is leading us to do. These are the **sins of omission.** We resist Him when we become stubborn and insensitive to Him. These are the **sins of submission.** But how do we know if we are guilty of any of these sins? We may have a general sense that there is a problem in our abiding if we recognize that fruit is lacking. We may even sense a lack of love or joy. Perhaps peace may be missing in our hearts. But how do we know what it is that has gotten in the way of our abiding?

The good news is that God loves us. He wants us to walk in fellowship with Him even more than we desire to do that. He is ready, willing, and able to show us if there is a problem in our relationship with Him. We don't have to go aimlessly looking for sin in a purely self-introspective way. Since the Spirit of God indwells us, we can trust that if we sincerely ask Him to, He will quickly reveal any issues in our lives that need to be addressed.

 Take a moment to pray through the areas listed below and ask God to bring to mind anything that is getting in the way of your abiding.

Sins of commission: Is there anything you are doing that the Lord has convicted you that you shouldn't be doing?

_____

_____

_____

Sins of omission: Is there anything you are not doing that you sense the Lord is asking you by His prompting and His Word to do?

_____

_____

_____

Did You Know?

FILLED OR BAPTIZED?

What is the difference between being "filled" with the Spirit and being "baptized" with the Spirit? Being filled can occur more than once and is not necessarily the experience of every believer, though it should be. We see the same group of people "filled" with the Spirit on multiple occasions in Acts. The baptism of the Spirit occurs only once, at salvation, and takes place in the life of every Christian. First Corinthians 12:13 states, *"For by one Spirit we were all baptized into one body . . . and we were all made to drink of one Spirit."*

Sins of submission: Is there any stubbornness or lack of sensitivity toward God in your heart, keeping you from being submitted to Him?

_____

_____

_____

_____

An Important Distinction: It is important when dealing with sin that we recognize the difference between the Holy Spirit's conviction and Satan's condemnation. Conviction is always very specific ("This is what you did wrong") and has repentance and restoration in view. Condemnation on the other hand, is always general ("You are a bad person") and has as its goal to keep you down and miserable. Conviction looks to the future (repentance and restoration). Condemnation, however, looks to the past (guilty emotions, feelings of failure and worthlessness, etc.). The apostle Paul explains what our attitude should be: _"Brethren, I do not regard myself as having laid hold of it yet_ [spiritual maturity]_, but one thing I do: forgetting what lies behind and reaching forward to what lies ahead, I press on toward the goal for the prize of the upward call of God in Christ Jesus"_ (Philippians 3:13–14). You don't have to live in past failures.

To be filled with the Spirit is a command in Ephesians 5:18, so we know it is God's will. If we sincerely ask God to fill us with His Spirit, and we confess any hinderances we are aware of to Him, then we can trust with confidence that He answers that prayer, regardless of whether or not we have some emotional experience. By faith, we can know that He fills us, for 1 John 5:14–15 tells us, _"This is the confidence which we have before Him, that, if we ask anything according to His will, He hears us. And if we know that He hears us in whatever we ask, we know that we have the requests which we have asked from Him."_

Why not take some time to express your heart to the Lord in writing. Tell Him what you desire in your relationship with Him. Thank Him for all He has done for you and is doing. Ask Him for the things for which you want to trust Him. Use the space below and write out your prayer to Him.

_____

_____

_____

_____

_____

_____

_____

_____

_____

_____

_____

_____

_____

> _Doctrine_
> ## CONVICTION AND CONDEMNATION
>
> Remember the difference between conviction and condemnation...
>
> **CONVICTION:**
> - ✓ what the Spirit does
> - ✓ is always specific
> - ✓ looks to the future
> - ✓ has the aim of repentance and restoration
> - ✓ produces hope
>
> **CONDEMNATION:**
> - ✓ what Satan does
> - ✓ is always general
> - ✓ looks to the past
> - ✓ has the aim of discouragement
> - ✓ produces hopelessness

Notes

Dealing with Sin

I can still remember the despair and disillusionment I felt the first time I really blew it and sinned in a big way after I had become a Christian. When I met Christ as a freshman in college, those first few months as a Christian were one great big honeymoon—a constant emotional high! In addition to going to church and participating in a Sunday school class, I got involved with every Christian activity on campus I could find, from the Baptist Student Union (BSU) to the Black Student Association Gospel Choir (I was the only white guy in there). I went to an interdenominational prayer meeting three days a week at 7:00 AM, was in a dorm Bible study, participated in Campus Crusade for Christ and the Christian Student House, and was part of a community Bible study, as well as any other form of Christian activity I could find. If it was Christian, I was there. I carried a New Testament in my back pocket, and read it between classes every time I had a spare minute. After developing friendships with a lot of other Christians, I even led several of my other friends to Christ. Everything seemed to be going great. I was enjoying my walk with Christ and was growing. And then, out of nowhere, I stumbled into an old sin habit. I knew it wasn't pleasing to the Lord, and frankly, I was shocked since I thought sin was a thing of the past. I was ashamed to tell anyone or ask for help.

Every time we sin, someone else is affected. Either they share in the bad that results, or they are robbed of the good that would have come if we had not sinned.

At first I was overwhelmed with guilt, but that faded in time. In its place was a sense of coldness in my walk with God. Soon I failed again, and felt even worse. I tried diligently to conquer temptations, but wasn't having much success. I began to notice that I no longer felt the same warmth and closeness in my relationship with Christ that I had known earlier. The more sin crept up in my life, the worse I felt about it. Sometimes I wondered if God even heard my prayers anymore. I wondered if I would ever be close to the Lord again. Maybe that was just for special times like retreats, or just for special people. Yet I had known such joy and victory for a season. After some time and with the help of some Christian friends, I learned that Christians aren't perfect yet, and that growth is a process. I had to come to grips with the principle of sin.

"Sin Happens." We wish it didn't but it does. We wish it disappeared once we became Christians, but that is not the case—at least not yet. You see, salvation is a progressive thing. The word "salvation" literally means "deliverance," and you and I are in the process of deliverance. We were delivered from the penalty of sin when we first trusted Christ. We are being delivered from the power of sin bit by bit as we grow in our relationship with Him. But we won't be delivered completely from the presence of sin until we leave this earth and get the glorified bodies we will have in heaven. In the meantime, we still have to deal with the fact that we sometimes sin. We saw in John 15:7–8 that one of the things that proves we are a disciple of Jesus is if we abide in Him. In this lesson we want to continue looking at the idea of abiding, but now from the aspect that keeps us from it. We want to look at how sin happens in the life of a believer, and what God wants done about it.

Dealing with Sin

> ### Did You Know?
> **A TRANSFORMED LIFE**
>
> Second Corinthians 3:18 tells us, *"But we all, with unveiled face beholding as in a mirror the glory of the Lord, are being transformed into the same image from glory to glory."* The Greek word for *"transformed"* is the word *metamorphóō* from which we get our English word "metamorphosis"—the scientific term for a caterpillar changing into a butterfly.

How Does Sin Happen?

We will probably sin, sooner or later, but we don't have to stay there. God has provided everything we need to enjoy uninterrupted fellowship with Him. Unfortunately, many Christians don't. They are either uninformed about God's love and forgiveness, or they don't understand that the cross affects the present as well as the past. Being a Christian doesn't mean that we cannot sin, but it does mean that when we do, we shouldn't stay there. A caterpillar can only crawl. That is all his nature allows him to do. But when he is changed into a butterfly, he can fly. Living in a whole new realm, he can still back and crawl on the ground, but he doesn't have to stay there anymore. He has wings now. In the same way a caterpillar changes into a butterfly, a new Christian experiences a transformation. He has been given access to a whole new way of living. He can go back to his old way of living, but he doesn't have to stay there. God wants to free us from those sinful, destructive habits of the old life. As we consider the sin principle, today we want to look at how sin happens. Understanding how we fall can help us avoid sin more often in the future. To do this, we want to go back and look at the very first sin.

One can only imagine what life was like in the Garden of Eden before sin. Adam and Eve had tasks to perform, but work was not by the sweat of the brow. They not only enjoyed intimacy with each other that was unstained by sin, but more importantly, they enjoyed unhindered intimacy with God. But Eve, having entered into a discussion with the serpent and having been deceived, gave in to temptation. As a result, everything changed—and not for the better. We want to start by looking at how Eve was tempted and see what we can learn about our own temptations.

📖 In Genesis 3:1 we see Eve engaging in a conversation with the serpent. Why, from what the text says about what he is like and what he does, is that a bad idea?

_____

_____

_____

_____

_____

The text reveals two negative realities about Satan: What he is like—"more crafty than any beast of the field. . . ."—and what he does—he calls into question the revealed will of God. He asks, "Indeed, has God said. . . ?" He also exaggerates the limitations that God's will imposed on mankind. He misquotes God as saying, "You shall not eat from any tree of the garden."

📖 There are several passages in the New Testament that give us some commentary on Eve's stumbling. Look at 2 Corinthians 11:3 and 12–15, and 1 Timothy 2:14, writing down what you learn about Satan's activities.

2 Corinthians 11:3

_____

_____

_____

2 Corinthians 11:12–15

_____

_____

_____

1 Timothy 2:14

_____

_____

_____

We see in 2 Corinthians 11:3 that the serpent "**deceived** _Eve by his craftiness_." This idea is also reinforced by Paul in 1 Timothy 2:14 where he says that she was "_quite deceived_." Satan (along with his workers) operates through deception and disguise. In fact, we are told in 2 Corinthians 11:14 that he "_disguises himself as an angel of light._" When dealing with an enemy who doesn't deal in truth, one must be especially careful to not take anything at face value. Eve should have let God's words be her authority, but as soon as Satan tricked her into calling what God said into question, it was only a matter of time before she went her own independent way. When we make ourselves the judge of whether God's words are true, transgression is inevitable.

When we make ourselves the judge of whether God's words are true, transgression is inevitable.

As you look closely at Eve's responses to Satan's questions, it looks at first like she accurately represents God's will, but if you look more closely, you will discover some important differences. Compare how Eve quotes God in Genesis 3:2–3 with what God actually says in Genesis 2:16–17. On the chart below, mark the differences you see and write your observations on what she adds and what she leaves out.

How Eve Quoted God (Genesis 3:2–3)	What God Said (Genesis 2:16–17)
From the fruit of the trees of the garden we may eat	From any tree of the garden you may eat freely
but from the fruit of the tree which is in the middle of the garden	but from the tree of the knowledge of good and evil
God has said, 'You shall not eat from it or touch it	you shall not eat
lest you die.'	for in the day that you eat from it you shall surely die.

Put Yourself In Their Shoes
EVE'S BIG MISTAKE

In quoting God, Eve...

• maximized the restrictions of the garden

• minimized the freedoms

• minimized the certainty of consequences for disobeying

It is incredibly revealing when we look closely at the subtle but significant differences in how Eve quotes God compared to what He actually said. God had actually instructed that Adam and Eve could eat *"From any tree. . . "* and that they *"may eat freely."* Both statements emphasize the liberty of the Garden. Eve, by leaving these out, seems to be minimizing or making light of her liberties. God's sole restriction in the Garden was specific—they were not to eat *"from the tree of the knowledge of good and evil."* Eve doesn't focus on what the tree is, but on where it is. She avoids the reminder that the tree is associated with evil. In restricting Adam and Eve, God had said only, *"You shall not eat."* Eve adds the phrase, *"or touch it,"* and in so doing, seems to maximize the restrictions or limitations God had placed on them in the Garden. Finally, Eve quotes the consequence as *"lest you die."* She leaves out the term *"surely,"* and the phrase *"in the day that you eat from it,"* apparently making light of the certainty and immediacy of the consequences. When we shade God's truth just a little bit, it can have disastrous impact.

How does sin happen? It happens when we begin to doubt the truthfulness of what God says. We need to learn from Eve how easy it is to major on the limitations God places and minor on the liberties He gives us.

Dealing with Sin   DAY TWO

WHY WE CHOOSE TO SIN

When Eve began her conversation with the serpent, she had no idea how far-reaching the consequences would be. Likewise, we often treat our own temptations with equal disregard. We fail to realize that sin has consequences that reach for generations. Every time I sin someone else is affected. They may be affected directly through some consequence of the sin, or they may be affected indirectly through the loss of the ministry and life I would have given if I had continued walking with God.

We learn painfully from Eve here that talking with the devil and walking with the Lord do not go hand in hand.

📖 Looking at Genesis 3:4–5, How does Satan cast doubt on the things God has said?

_____

_____

_____

_____

Satan calls into question two significant things in these verses. First, by saying, _"You surely shall not die,"_ he casts doubt on the truthfulness of what God said. Second, by saying, _"For God knows that in the day you eat from it your eyes will be opened, and you will be like God, knowing good and evil,"_ Satan invites Eve to doubt the goodness of God's motives. He suggests that God is withholding something good from Eve. The Bible says that whatever is not from faith is sin (Romans 14:23). All sin is rooted in a lack of faith. We choose our own way, because we doubt that what God wants for us is really for our best. We somehow think that we know better than He does how to make ourselves happy and fulfilled.

📖 Satan attacked Eve with a strategy, but that strategy really hasn't changed much over the years. Compare Genesis 3:6 with 1 John 2:16 and identify the parallels in Satan's temptation today.

"The lust of the flesh"

_____

_____

"The lust of the eyes"

_____

_____

"The boastful pride of life"

_____

_____

> _"But he who doubts is condemned if he eats, because he does not eat from faith; for whatever is not from faith is sin."_
>
> **Romans 14:23**

Looking closely at Genesis 3:6 in the light of 1 John, the parallel is obvious. The statement, _"When the woman saw that the tree was good for food,"_ would seem to correlate with _"the lust of the flesh."_ The phrase, _"and that it was a delight to the eyes,"_ connects directly with _"the lust of the eyes."_ Finally, the phrase, _"and that the tree was desirable to make one wise,"_ appears to be the same issue as _"the boastful pride of life."_ It would seem that all temptation could be traced to these three enticements (sensualism, materialism, and pride [see also Jesus' temptation in the wilderness in Matthew 4]). The sin in the Garden was more than eating forbidden fruit, it was disobeying the revealed Word of God, believing the lies of the enemy, and Adam and Eve placing their own will above God's will.

How do we sin? It starts when we are willing to doubt the truth of what God says and to doubt the goodness of His motives toward us. If you will think back on the last time you sinned, you will find those two mistakes somewhere in the process. Why do Christians commit immorality? Because they don't believe that such an act will have the consequences God says it will have, and because they doubt that doing it God's way will really make them happier. They aren't willing to wait for what God provides. We sin because we doubt that what God says is true, and we don't believe He has our best interests at heart.

Dealing with Sin **DAY THREE**

THE WRONG WAY TO DEAL WITH SIN WHEN IT HAPPENS

The problem of the Garden begins with the forbidden fruit, but it does not end there. In fact, it would seem from the continuation of the story that the consequences of Genesis 3 have as much to do with how Adam and Eve responded to their failure as with the failure itself. Having a heart after God's heart is not the absence of failure, but the willingness to deal with failure in a biblical way. Today we want to examine more closely the problems with how Adam and Eve dealt with their failure.

📖 Look at Genesis 3:7–8 and identify Adam and Eve's first approach to dealing with their sin.

_____

_____

_____

_____

Adam and Eve's problems were not just that they rebelled, but that when confronted with their rebellion, they failed to deal with it the right way.

We see in verse 7 that Adam and Eve start by hiding from each other. They try to cover their nakedness with fig leaves. Next, in verse 8, they try to hide from God among the trees of the Garden (where they should have stayed in the first place). It is our natural response of the flesh to try to hide when we sin. Pride never wants to be found out. Humility, on the other hand, is quick to take responsibility for failure. In Adam and Eve, we see ourselves and our tendency to hide when we sin. It is this very tendency that alienates us from other believers and from God, and which gets in the way of putting the sin behind us. One of the biggest things that keep us stuck in sin is that we can't admit it to anyone. We want to be perfect; we know we aren't; so we try to hide our imperfections. That very action of hiding keeps us from progressing.

Fortunately, God will not let our hiding succeed. Nothing is hidden from Him. By His Spirit who lives in us, He convicts and confronts the sins we try to hide. He doesn't do this to make us miserable. He does it so He can help us out of the pit we have fallen into. He wants to put us back on the right path so we can enjoy His blessing. Just as God came to Adam and Eve, He comes to us, but He does not force Himself. God asked Adam, "Where are you?" He knew where Adam was, but He wanted to give Adam the chance to admit where He was—to come out of hiding. Unfortunately, hiding was not the only mistake Adam and Eve made in dealing with their sin. God confronted Adam and Eve and asked if they had eaten of the forbidden fruit. But instead of taking responsibility for their sin, they tried to pass the buck.

📖 Look at where Adam and Eve place blame for their sin (Genesis 3:12–13). What can we learn from this about our own tendencies in dealing with sin?

_____

_____

_____

_____

Put Yourself In Their Shoes
THE BLAME GAME

Adam and Eve dealt wrongly with their sin by…

• trying to hide it

• trying to blame it on others

We see in Adam's response that with one statement he tries to shift the blame for his sin to both Eve and God. He says, *"the woman* (blaming Eve) *whom You gave to be with me . . ."* (blaming God). Eve takes the same approach, for she tries to shift the blame onto Satan (*"the serpent deceived me"*). Our human tendency is to blame someone else, instead of taking responsibility for our sins. This too, gets in the way of progress.

We sin because of unbelief, doubting the truth of what God says and the goodness of what He wants. We stay stuck in sin because we deal with it the wrong way, trying to hide it from others and from God. Then we try to blame our sin on others. But "hide and seek" and the "blame game" get us nowhere—but stuck.

APPLY Can you think of any examples in your own life where these principles have manifested themselves?

_____

_____

_____

_____

While playing games with God about our sin can get us stuck, fortunately there is a way out. Tomorrow we want to look at the right way to deal with sin. But first, we want to look at what King David wrote about what happens when we deal with sin the wrong way.

📖 Read Psalm 32:3–4. What consequences did David face for hiding his sin?

_____

_____

_____

CONSEQUENCES OF HIDING SIN

"When I kept silent, my bones grew old through my groaning all the day long. For day and night Your hand was heavy upon me; my vitality was turned into the drought of summer. Selah"

When David kept silent about his sin (kept it hidden), even though he thought no one knew about it, God knew. Nothing is hidden from God. David's unconfessed sin affected him even physically as his body wasted away. God's hand heavy upon Him, David felt the immense weight of his guilt. His vitality (his joy and his energy for life) was drained away. We can try to keep our sin hidden, or even when it is exposed, try to hide behind blaming someone or something else for it. But God will not let our hiding succeed. He loves us too much to not deal with the sickness of sin, for He knows unresolved sin won't just go away by itself. He convicts us of sin, not to tell us how bad we are, but to tell us how forgiven we are and to tell us we can be free from that old, fruitless way of living. "Hide and seek" may have been a fun game when we were children, but God wants us as Christians to grow up and stop playing games with our sin.

Sin happens even to the best of us. One of the godliest men in the Old Testament was King David. He was called "a man after God's heart." He was a good leader and a good example. But still, he sinned. In fact, he probably sinned far worse than anything you have ever done. He committed both adultery and murder. While his troops were off at war, he had an affair with his neighbor, Bathsheba. When she became pregnant, he had her husband killed in battle to cover up their sin. What made David a man after God's heart was not that he was perfect, but that he kept coming back to God with a heart of humility, seeking forgiveness and cleansing. The question for which David has the right answer is "Why deal with sin?"

📖 We saw the consequences of hiding our sins. Read Psalm 32:1–2 and 5. What results when we confess our sins to the Lord?

_____

_____

_____

_____

When we confess our sins, we get to experience all of the benefits of forgiveness. We are *"blessed"* (the word means "fully satisfied"). Our spirit is no longer clouded with deceit. When we stop hiding our sin from God and confess it to Him, not only does He forgive us, but He also takes away the guilt as well. We can again enjoy all the benefits of His loving fellowship!

Dealing with Sin | DAY FOUR |

THE RIGHT WAY TO DEAL WITH SIN

Sin is the barrier that gets in the way of a fleshly believer experiencing the love and forgiveness God offers. God loves us unconditionally, so His love for us does not change when we sin. Just as the sun is always shining even when clouds obstruct our view of it, His love is always manifested toward His children even when they don't feel it. Sometimes we feel that Jesus forgave the sins we committed before we became Christians, but after that, we are on our own. We feel He is able to deal with the sins of the past, but not the sins of the future. But since Jesus died on the cross for our sins two thousand years ago, then in order for Him to deal with any of our sins, He had to deal with all of them, for all our sins were still in the future when He died for them. Because all of our sins were forgiven on the cross, you may be asking, "Then why do they break my fellowship with God?" That is a good question. Simply put, the answer lies in the fact that every sin is a straying from God. He still loves us, but we have moved away from Him. In order to experience the benefits of His love and forgiveness, we must return to Him.

📖 Read Luke 15:11–24. Write down in your own words the basic points of the story.

_____

_____

_____

In Luke 15, Jesus told a story of a son who left home with his inheritance and wasted all his money on wild living. When the money was gone, a famine hit the land, and the only job he could find was feeding pigs. What a humiliating job for a Jew who considered pigs unclean! In fact, things were so bad, the pigs were eating better than he was. He began to remember the wonderful meals he had eaten at his father's house and how much his father loved him. The admission of his self-destruction combined with fond memories of his father's love for him prompted the son to return home. When he neared his father's house, the father saw him and ran to him. His father embraced him repeatedly and called his servants to put the best robe on him and prepare for a party. His son had returned! If the son had really understood his father's love, he would not have stayed away so long. So too, for us.

Jesus told this parable we call "The Prodigal Son" to teach us how God views us. Personally, I think the title we have given this story is the wrong one, for the son is not the central figure. The main point of the story is not the son's straying, but the father's love. I think we ought to call the parable, "The Loving Father." He is the first one mentioned in the story: *"A certain man had two sons. . . ."* To appreciate all this story teaches about how God wants us to deal with sin, we must look at it a little more closely.

📖 Consider Luke 15:14–16, and write your thoughts on how God encouraged the son to go home and how God helps us to return to Him.

_____

_____

_____

It is a sobering reality that God will not let His children stay in sin and enjoy it. There is a passing pleasure to sin (Hebrews 11:25), but it does not last. The most miserable person on earth is not the unbeliever (his misery comes later), but the believer who is not walking with God. A Christian can enjoy God, and a non-Christian can enjoy sin, but a straying Christian can enjoy neither. His sin keeps him from enjoying God, and God living in him keeps him from enjoying his sin. God brought a famine to the land so that the son could not keep enjoying his sin. God didn't do this to punish him, but to bring him to his senses. His own need drove him home. God treats us this same way.

📖 Look at Luke 15:17–19. Compare how the son plans on returning to the father with how we tend to come to God after we have sinned.

_____

_____

_____

_____

_____

Circumstances made the straying son come to his senses. As he reflected, he thought, *Even the hired servants in my father's house are faring better than I am right now.* He decided to return and beg his father's forgiveness. Surely he thought, *He can never forgive me for the foolish thing I have done, but maybe he will hire me as a servant.* How wrong was this son's understanding of his

In Luke 15, Jesus tells three parables with a common theme: the shepherd who loses his sheep; the woman who loses her coin; and the father who loses his son. In each case, someone longs for the recovery of that which was lost, and rejoices greatly when it is found.

Often we try to return to God after we have sinned as if His forgiveness places us on probation.

father's love! No loving father could ever take a wandering son back as a slave. Yet in the same way, often we try to return to God after we have sinned as if His forgiveness places us on probation. In other words, we mistakenly assume that He will accept us back, but we'd better tow the line from here on out! We don't understand that God views us as His children, not slaves. We could not earn His love and forgiveness, no matter how long we labored to do so. Our future faithfulness is an expression of gratitude for His love, but has no power to earn His love.

📖 Looking at Luke 15:20–24, how does the son's returning home compare with our returning to God after sin?

_____

_____

_____

_____

Did You Know?
THE SIGNET RING

The ring the father had his servants place on the prodigal son's hand was a signet ring. It consisted of a family crest or symbol. It could be used much like a credit card. When its emblem was imprinted in hot wax, it enabled the possessor to make purchases with the full credit of the family who was represented.

When the son made a move toward the father, the Father ran to him. What an awesome picture this is of God's love toward us! The story tells us the father saw the son *"while he was still a long way off."* For this to happen, the father had to be looking for him. When we stray from God, He is ever looking for our return, and He rejoices greatly when we do so! Not only that, but He restores us to the family, not to the household staff. He clothes us in royal robes to replace the sin-stained garments from our wandering with the world. He restores us to the position of rightful heir.

How do we deal with sin? The same way the prodigal son did. If you look closely at the story, you will find three correct parts to the son's return. These are the things he did right. He remembered; he recognized; and he repented. His return began when he remembered what it was like in the father's house. For us to return to God begins with remembering what it is like to be in fellowship with God. Secondly, not only did the son remember the father's house, but he also recognized his sin. He said, *"I have sinned against heaven and in your sight."* He recognized that his actions had offended both God and man. When we sin, we must confess that sin to God and ask His forgiveness, but often there are people we need to seek forgiveness from as well. Thirdly, repentance was required. Repentance means to have a change of mind that produces a change of action. The son turned his back on his father when he squandered his estate on loose living. But when he returned to the father's house, he turned his back on his wandering ways. Those same three steps are necessary for us in dealing with sin. We must remember our relationship with God; we must recognize what is wrong; and we must turn from our sin back to our Father.

Dealing with Sin

FOR ME TO FOLLOW GOD

In 1 Corinthians 10:11 we are told, *"Now these things happened to them as an example, and they were written for our instruction, upon whom the ends of the ages have come."* We must recognize that the biographical sketch of Adam and Eve we have just studied in Scripture is not simply a matter of history, but is written for our instruction. This means their lives make demands on our lives. We must be willing to ask the hard question, "How do Adam and Eve apply to me today?" We can ask the same question regarding the mistakes of King David and the parable of the prodigal son. If we weave these three biblical lessons together, we have a pretty good picture not only of how sin happens, but also how we deal with it—both correctly and incorrectly.

APPLY As you consider your own walk with God, think about the last time you sinned. Can you see some examples in your own experience that mirror the mistakes of Adam and Eve in the garden?

_____

_____

_____

Earlier in this lesson on sin, we saw in 2 Corinthians 11:3 that the crux of spiritual warfare is all about Satan trying to lead us astray from *"the simplicity and purity of devotion to Christ."* If he can do that by tempting us to rebel, he is happy. But he is just as happy if he can tempt us to be religious instead of walking with God. He doesn't mind our striving in religion—so long as we stay away from relationship. With Satan, anything is fine that keeps us from devoting our lives to Christ.

When Adam and Eve sinned, part of their problem was not just what they did wrong, but how they wrongly dealt with their sin. Can you think of some examples in your life or others you know of trying to hide sin?

_____

_____

_____

What about trying to blame others for sin?

_____

_____

_____

_____

Sin that is hidden from others is not hidden from God or from our own hearts. It corrodes our joy and weighs down our hearts. Our joy and hearts are affected because God has placed within us a conscience that condemns us when we are wrong. Blaming others for sin may make us feel better for a time, for it may ease our conscience to think our wrong choices were someone else's fault. But no one can make us sin. First Corinthians 10:13 promises that God will not allow us to be tempted beyond what we are able to bear. The down side of that is that when we give in, we can't blame anyone but ourselves for our choices. Others may have made those choices easier for us, but if the choice was more than our faith could handle, God would not allow the temptation to come to us. When we fail to be obedient, it isn't that we can't resist, but that we chose not to resist. Blaming others doesn't take away our responsibility for the choices we make. Often, when we blame others for our choices, the result is that we become bitter toward them. This may cloud us from seeing our own responsibility. Hiding sin doesn't work, and neither does blaming others for it. The only way to deal with sin is God's way.

> "But I am afraid, lest as the serpent deceived Eve by his craftiness, your minds should be led astray from the simplicity and purity of devotion to Christ."
>
> **2 Corinthians 11:3**

APPLY In the story of the prodigal son and his loving father, we saw three principles on how to return when we have sinned. Reflect on these principles and any application you find to your own situation.

Remember

Remember what it is like in the father's house, what it is like to walk in close fellowship with God. Write down what stands out to you of being close to God.

_____

_____

_____

Recognize

Recognize what is sin in your life—whether it be sins in what you have done, in what you have not done, and in not being submitted to God.

_____

_____

_____

_____

Repent

Repentance means turning from one thing and turning to another. What do you need to turn from? What do you need to turn toward?

_____

_____

_____

📖 Read 1 John 1:9. What does it promise will happen when we confess our sins?

_____

_____

_____

 *Doctrine*
CONFESSING SIN

The Old and the New Testaments reveal the same truths. We are to agree with God about our sin. In 1 John 1:9, we find these words, *"If we confess our sins, He is faithful and righteous to forgive us our sins and to cleanse us from all unrighteousness."* The Greek word for "confess" (*homologeō*) means "to say the same thing." We are to say the same thing about our sin as God says. He says it is wrong. It is to be forsaken. It has been forgiven. When we confess, we draw His forgiveness and cleansing into our daily experience.

If we confess our sins, God is faithful both to forgive the penalty of the sin, and to cleanse the sinner. The slate is wiped clean. It is important to understand what it means to confess. The word "confess" literally means "to say the same thing" or "to agree." When we confess our sins, we are agreeing with God's view of our sins. We are not telling Him something He doesn't already know. He knows everything. Confession is not for His benefit, but for ours. We need to come to grips with what is wrong. When we confess our sins, we are agreeing that what God says is wrong really is wrong. That is why true confession always is accompanied by repentance. If we aren't willing to turn our back on the sin, then we really don't believe it is sin. We must agree that the action is wrong, but we must also agree that the action is forgiven. We should thank God that Jesus died for that sin.

Many of us still walk loaded down with guilt as a result of sins we have committed. We agree that they are wrong, but we have never agreed with God that they are forgiven. As an application of this lesson, take out a separate sheet of paper. On that sheet, write down every sin that God brings to mind.

You don't need to become introspective, looking for sin in every action or attitude. Just invite the Lord to search your heart and bring to mind anything that is unresolved. That is what David did in Psalm 139:23–24: *"Search me, O God, and know my heart; Try me and know my anxious thoughts; And see if there be any hurtful way in me."* Whatever the Lord brings to mind write it down. Once you feel you are done, write 1 John 1:9 across the page. Then as a marker in your own mind, burn the sheet of paper as a reminder that God considers those sins gone. Thank Him for His love and forgiveness!

You may want to close out this week's lesson by writing a prayer of thankfulness for His love and forgiveness that you can come back to again and again. Use the space provided below.

_____

_____

_____

_____

_____

_____

_____

_____

_____

_____

Notes

step five

Bible Study

The goal of the Christian life is to be a faithful disciple or follower of Jesus. We saw in John 15:7–8 that to be a disciple, we must abide in Him. We also saw that His Word must abide in us. This week we will begin looking at the principle of Bible study. The Word of God stands alone as the most unique book in history, one written over a period of thousands of years by some forty different authors from all walks of life. It was written by kings and shepherds, fishermen and farmers. And yet the theme is incredibly consistent, as we look at its sixty-six different books. How could men from different times, different places, different cultures, different walks of life, weave together such sublime words of wisdom? Peter explains: *"But know this first of all, that no prophecy of Scripture is a matter of one's own interpretation, for no prophecy was ever made by an act of human will, but men moved by the Holy Spirit spoke from God."* (2 Peter 1:20–21). Though He used many different people as His pens, God is the author of the Bible. It is His work and His words.

It is an amazing thought that God has written a book. Think of how important an issue that is in faith. It is yet another way that God has stooped down to communicate Himself in a way we could understand. John Wesley, founder of the Methodist Church, wrote:

I am a creature of a day, passing through life as an arrow through the air. I am a spirit coming from God and returning to God, hovering over the great gulf. A few months hence I am no more seen. I drop into an unchangeable eternity. I want to know one thing— if God Himself has condescended to teach the way. He hath written it down in a book. . . . Oh, give me that book! At any price, give me the book of God!

Bible Study   **DAY ONE**   # WHAT THE WORD OF GOD IS ABLE TO DO

To understand the importance of the Word of God in our lives, we must have a sense of all it is able to do for us and in us. Using the chart below, look up the verses listed and record what they teach about the **nature of the Word** in the column in the center, and what they teach about the **benefits of the Word** in the column on the right. Not every verse will have something for both columns, so if the particular subject isn't addressed, leave that space blank.

PASSAGE	NATURE OF THE WORD	BENEFITS OF THE WORD
Psalm 19:7a	Perfect	(Refreshes) Revives the Soul
Psalm 19:7b	Trustworthy	Makes Wise- seeing things from Gods perspective
Psalm 19:8a	Right	Gives joy to the heart ↑ peace, contentment
Psalm 19:8b	Radiant	Gives understanding - opens our eyes to truth
Psalm 19:9a	Pure	obedient respect toward God
Psalm 19:9b	Reliable/ altogether righteous	Dependable
Psalm 19:10	Desirable ; Precious ; Pleasant	
Psalm 19:11		
Psalm 19:12	Reveals hidden faults	Encourages us to ask forgiveness
Psalm 19:13	Prevents us from doing what we know is wrong.	Keeps us from being controlled by sin.
Psalm 19:14		Words pleasing to God.

Psalm 19 paints an awesome portrait of the Word of God. Look at the terms it uses to describe the nature of Scripture. God's law is perfect—it is flawless and free from blemish. The Lord's testimony is sure—firm and able to support us. His precepts are right—they are straight and upright. God's commandment is pure—unstained and without error. It is clean—the Hebrew word has the idea of being unalloyed. Nothing else is mixed in. The judgments of the Lord are true—the Hebrew word for true speaks of firmness and stability. God's truths are more desirable than gold and sweeter than honey. These statements are all focused on what God's Word offers and is able to do in our lives. The Scriptures can restore our souls—our inner man, and can make wise the simple-minded, give joy to the heart and enlighten our way. In addition, these truths of God last forever and are altogether righteous. They can warn us, but also point us toward reward as we obey what they say. The Scriptures can help us discern error, guard us from sinning intentionally, and so work in our hearts that our words and thoughts become pleasing to God. What a book is this book of books! A German dramatist described his relationship to the Word of God like this: "I have read many books, but the Bible stands alone—it reads me."

READING: THE BEGINNING OF BIBLE STUDY

Bible Study DAY TWO

One of the most incredible realities of the Word of God is that every time we read, it speaks afresh. Even in the truths we understand, we have need of being reminded, for our call is not simply to understand truth but to live it. The great evangelist, D. L. Moody put it this way: "The only way to keep a broken vessel full is to keep the faucet running." Thus, we need to read and study God's Word over and over. But how do we do that practically? How do we let His words abide in us? The rest of this lesson is devoted to practical ways we can fulfill this part of being a disciple.

For the words of Jesus to "abide" in us, we must spend much time with them. The term "abide" conveys the idea of being at home in us. Colossians 3:16 tells us, *"Let the word of Christ richly dwell within you."* It goes on to explain that when His word dwells in us, we will teach and admonish others with wisdom. But does this mean I have to go to seminary and learn to speak Greek and Hebrew? Many people wrongly believe that Bible study is something akin to what we see a stunt driver do on television. It comes with the disclaimer, "Don't try this at home." We fear that to really understand the Bible, we must be an ivory tower intellectual or a monk locked up in some ancient castle. Well, maybe an intellectual or a devout monk can glean much from their study of the Scriptures, but so can you. Remember, we saw in Psalm 19:7 that God's word can *"mak[e] wise the simple."* The Bible is an inexhaustible source of wisdom and knowledge. The more we study it, the more we can learn. But it reaches down to right where we are. Studying the Bible doesn't begin with parsing Greek verbs with dusty textbooks. It begins simply by reading.

During the reign of King Josiah, a great revival came to the people of Judah. His father, Amon, and his grandfather, Manasseh, had led God's people astray into idol worship. The Temple of God had fallen into disrepair. But Josiah became a reformer. Through his leadership, and the godly influence of believers around him, the Temple was cleaned and repaired. In the process, someone discovered a copy of the Scriptures. So neglected was the spiritual life of the nation, that no one even knew what the Bible said. Yet this discovery would bring great change.

📖 Read 2 Chronicles 34:14–21. How did Josiah respond when the Bible was found and read to him?

He tore his robes, He realized that God's Word had not been kept

How can we know what pleases or displeases God apart from His Word? Josiah and many of the people in Judah did not necessarily have evil in their hearts. Yet their lives were not what they should have been. Once the Word of God was read, Josiah fell under conviction. He recognized things that were wrong in the nation. He saw their sin. When he tore his robes, that action was a sign in his culture of repentance and mourning over sin. As he saw God's heart reflected in the Scriptures, his own heart was moved.

📖 Second Kings 23:1–3 records more of Josiah's response. What changes did Josiah make because of the reading of God's Word?

He renewed the covenant.

Notice what Josiah did. His first action was to call the elders of Judah and Jerusalem to a meeting at the Temple. The people of Judah and Jerusalem went along with him as well as the priests and prophets. Having little to say, Josiah simply began reading the words of the book of the covenant (probably the first five books of the Bible which were authored by Moses). After he made an impassioned personal and public commitment to follow the Lord and His Word, the people followed his lead and entered into that covenant. Revival came to the nation, and all it took was the reading of the Word of God. No lengthy sermons were preached. No scholars tried to dissect each phrase. The Word was simply read, and it began to work.

Lest you think the experience of Josiah an isolated event, we want to consider another example of the power of reading the Word of God.

📖 Look at Nehemiah 8:1–18. How did the people of God respond to Ezra reading the Scriptures in each of the verses listed below?

Verse 3

Listened attentively

Verse 6

Worshipped the Lord

Verse 9

They wept/mourned.

Verse 12

They ate and drank + celebrated.

Verses 14–17

Made booths to dwell in
Rejoiced greatly

God's Word had been neglected. But through the initiative of Ezra, the Scriptures were read publicly to the people. Consider how they responded. In verse 3, we see that they were attentive to the book being read. The more they understood, the more it affected them. Verse 6 tells us they shouted "Amen!" and lifted their hands to the Lord. Then they bowed low and worshiped the Lord with their faces to the ground in respect for His holiness. As they heard the neglected words of God, they began to weep (verse 9). But after their grieving came great joy and celebration as they understood what had been read. They even reinstated the observance of the Feast of Booths that had been neglected since the days of Joshua. They saw what God wanted, and they were moved to obey. The end result of all of this was that _"there was great rejoicing"_ (verse 17). All this happened because the Bible was read.

You don't have to have a seminary degree to read your Bible. You just need to make time for it. I would encourage you to begin reading your Bible in a regular and systematic fashion. Maybe you can start with the Gospel of Matthew and read a bit each day until you finish the New Testament. That is what I did when I first became a Christian. I had a little Gideon New Testament that I had picked up a few days before I met Christ. I kept it in my back pocket and read whenever I had some time to spare. I would read a few verses or a few chapters. Each time God would have something to say. When I finished Matthew I moved on to Mark, Luke, and John. I kept on going. At first, I didn't have any set time. I just had the goal of discovering all that God had to say. Soon I developed the habit of reading a chapter or two when I got up in the morning and again when I went to bed. You may find that one of those times works best for your schedule and lifestyle, or perhaps during your lunch break is another option. The main point is not when you do it, but that you do it and do it regularly.

Although I began my Bible studies by reading the King James Version, I was pleased to discover some of the more modern translations that are written in language that is much easier to understand. Two of the better English translations, in my opinion, are the New American Standard Bible (NASB) and the New International Version (NIV). My first Easter as a Christian, my mother wanted to encourage me in my faith, so she went to a Christian bookstore with me and bought me an easy-to-read Bible. What a blessing that was for my fledgling faith! I encourage you to find a version you are

Did You Know?

MORE FACTS ABOUT THE BIBLE

Here are some more interesting tidbits concerning God's written Word:

- Number of verses—31,102
- Number of words—775,693
- Longest chapter (176 verses)— Psalm 119
- Shortest chapter (2 verses)— Psalm 117
- Longest verse—Esther 8:9
- Shortest verse—John 11:35
- Longest book in OT—Psalms
- Longest book in NT—Luke

comfortable with and start working your way through the Bible. I recommend starting with the New Testament, but you will find many wonderful things in the Old Testament as well. On page 173, you will find a New Testament reading schedule.

On page 173, you will find a New Testament reading schedule.

STUDYING THE BIBLE DILIGENTLY

It is a powerful thing to realize all that God can do in our lives when we just read His Word. But reading is the beginning, not the end. Imagine you are standing on the shore of a beautiful, deserted beach in the Bahamas. You look out over the pristine, azure water and think, "How beautiful!" Now, imagine that you put on a snorkel mask and dive in. The surface of the Caribbean is beautiful, but once you dive beneath the surface you find it is more beautiful still. You discover that there is so much more to be seen than just the water and the waves. You begin to see the incredible diversity of fish with so many different shapes and colors. You see the majestic beauty of coral reefs that took generations to take shape. The Word of God is like that. You read it and see its beauty, but the more you study it, the more beauty you discover.

📖 Read Romans 11:33–36 and write down what you learn there.

God's wisdom + knowledge is deep - we can never reach the bottom.

Paul speaks here of the *"depth of the riches . . . of the wisdom and knowledge of God."* The word he uses for "depth" is the Greek word, *bathos*, from which we get our English term "bathosphere," a submarine designed to be used at great depths. Paul goes on to say God's judgments are unsearchable and His ways unfathomable. These words do not mean that we cannot learn anything of God, but that we can never learn everything about God. Bible Study is not a fruitless search, for we find riches at every level. But the deeper we go, the more riches we find. The wisdom and knowledge of God are a treasure chest beyond imagining, and no matter how deep we dig, we never reach the bottom.

📖 Look at Psalm 111:2. What is a right response to God's workings according to this verse?

Delight/pleasure

If we take delight in the works of God, then they will be studied by us. We won't be satisfied with a surface understanding. The Hebrew word for "studied" here literally means, "sought out." There is a logical progression in what we are considering in this lesson. We start by reading God's Word, but as we are gripped by it, we are motivated to stop and study it.

📖 Consider Acts 17:11–12. What made the Jews of Berea *"more noble-minded"*?

> Examined the Scriptures to see
> if what Paul said was true.

What set the people of Berea apart was not just that they received the words of Paul with great eagerness, but also that they were willing to examine the Scriptures for themselves to check out what he had to say. The word "examine" has the idea of study. Verse 12 goes on to indicate that many of them took their studies to the next step after that—they were willing to act on what they were learning. They were willing to receive the Word, then to study it, and then to apply it.

How do we study the Word of God? An important thing to remember is that if it took the illumining work of God's Spirit for men to write Scripture, it will take that same illumining work for us to understand it. Bible study begins by asking God to help us understand His Word. But it also requires effort and integrity on our part.

📖 Look at 2 Timothy 2:15 and write what you learn.

> Study the Word so that you
> can correctly handle God's Word.

Paul exhorts Timothy to be diligent to make sure he handles God's Word accurately. The implied message in this is that it is actually possible to mishandle God's Word. Bible verses are like prisoners of war—if you torture them long enough you can get them to confess almost anything. But we don't want to be guilty of making the Bible say what we want it to say. We want to understand what it really means. To do this requires diligence in how we handle Scripture.

Some principles for handling the Bible correctly are. . .

✓ Make sure you understand the **context** of the verse you are studying. Sometimes we misunderstand a verse's message because we don't look at the verses around it.

✓ Make sure you look at each verse in light of the **complete** Word. Often confusion about what a verse says can be cleared up by comparing it to what the Bible teaches about that subject elsewhere.

✓ Try to find out what you can about the **culture** that affects what you are studying. Sometimes understanding the culture and history surrounding a passage makes all the difference in understanding fully what that passage teaches.

✓ Look at Bible verses in the light of the **character** of God. Each truth the Bible teaches is consistent with an accurate understanding of who God is.

"Now these [Jewish exiles of Berea] were more noble-minded than those in Thessalonica, for they received the word with great eagerness, examining the Scriptures daily, to see whether these things were so."

Acts 17:11

> *"To me, the Bible is alive, it speaks to me; it has feet, it runs after me; it has hands, it lays hold of me."*
>
> **—Martin Luther**

✓ Read the Bible, looking first for a **common sense** interpretation. The Bible was written to be understood. We take its statements literally unless it is clear that they are allegory or figurative statements.

Some helpful tools to guide you in looking for these things are. . .

✓ **An exhaustive Bible concordance:** this will help you locate other verses that use a key word or phrase. Make sure it fits the translation of the Bible you are reading.

✓ **A Bible dictionary:** often this will give you added cultural information on a topic. *Unger's Bible Dictionary* (Moody Press) is a good one.

✓ **A good study Bible:** this will give you help from respected Christian scholars in answering questions that naturally arise from your study. I recommend the *Ryrie Study Bible* (Moody Press), the *MacArthur Study Bible* (Thomas Nelson Publishers), and the *Key Word Study Bible* (AMG Publishers) as good choices.

You can pick these up at your local Christian bookstore. Another important and helpful tool in studying the Bible is found in resources like the book you are currently holding in your hands. A good Bible study book doesn't just tell you what to believe but takes you to the Bible so you can discover truth for yourself.

Bible Study **DAY FOUR**

APPLICATION: THE LOGICAL RESULT OF BIBLE STUDY

James, the brother of Jesus, wrote one of the books of the New Testament. In it he makes an important statement about studying the Bible. He says, *"But prove yourselves doers of the word, and not merely hearers who delude themselves"* (James 1:22). We study the Bible for more than just information. Our goal should be transformation. What we learn ought to affect how we live. James warns us that if we learn and do not apply what we learn, that information can become a deluding influence in our lives. It deceives us into thinking we are spiritual because of what we know instead of because of how we live. Today we will look at how we can draw out application from the passages we study.

📖 Read 2 Timothy 3:16–17.

For what is the Bible useful?

teaching
rebuking
correcting
Training

What is the result of studying the Bible?

Thoroughly equipped for every good work ... being a blessing to others.

This passage teaches us that the Bible is useful for *"teaching," "reproof," "correction,"* and *"training in righteousness."* In other words, these are the ways the Bible benefits us. As a result of studying the Bible properly, we become *"adequate"* and *"equipped"* for good works. The word *"adequate"* means "sufficient" or "complete"—we become a whole person. The second result is that we are equipped for good works. We become able to be a blessing to others.

To fully appreciate what this passage teaches about the applications of Scripture, it is important to understand the key terms. Look these words up in a dictionary to see more fully what they mean.

Teaching

_____
_____
_____
_____

Reproof

_____
_____
_____
_____

Correction

_____
_____
_____
_____

Training

_____
_____
_____
_____

"All Scripture is inspired by God and profitable for teaching, for reproof, for correction, for training in righteousness; that the man of God may be adequate, equipped for every good work."

—2 Timothy 3:16–17

Even just understanding the English terms is helpful, but it is even more helpful to know what the original words that Paul used here mean. These Greek words were translated to their closest equivalent in English, but the original language is more clear. The word for teaching (*didaskalia*) is also translated *"doctrine."* It literally means instruction, but also has the idea of what we need to believe. The word reproof (*elegchos*) means conviction—to show us what is wrong in our lives. The word correction (*epanorthōsis*) has the idea of making straight or setting right again. The Bible doesn't just show us where we are wrong, but shows us how to be right. The word for training (*paideia*) originally referred to the upbringing of children and has the idea of helping us to grow up spiritually into a righteous person. This is what the Bible can do in our lives—yes, even in your life!

As you consider these four things for which Scripture is useful, realize that these also show us the applications we ought to seek as we study the Bible. First of all, we need to look at a passage and ask, "What do I need to believe?" Belief determines behavior. What we believe about ourselves and about God is so important. Scripture shows us what we ought to believe about who we are, where we came from, and where we are headed. One type of application is simply *"teaching"* us what to believe. The second term, *"reproof,"* shows us to look for things the Bible may reveal that are wrong in our lives. If we are unwilling to change, we will never grow and become more than what we are. We must look to the Bible with humility, being willing to see when it reveals things that aren't right. We should ask, "Is there any sin I need to confess?" The third term, *"correction,"* guides us to look for what the Bible teaches about how to make right what is wrong. It should prompt us to ask, "What do I need to do differently?" Finally, *"training"* guides us to look more long term. "How can I make this a part of my life?" Choices produce habits, and habits result in character.

D. L. Moody said, "I prayed for faith and thought that some day faith would come down and strike me like lightening. But faith did not seem to come. One day I read in the tenth chapter of Romans, 'Now faith comes by hearing, and hearing by the Word of God.' I had closed my Bible and prayed for faith. I now opened my Bible and began to study, and faith has been growing ever since."

Bible Study | DAY FIVE

FOR ME TO FOLLOW GOD

In 1 Peter 2:1–3 we read, *"Therefore, putting aside all malice and all guile and hypocrisy and envy and all slander, like newborn babes, long for the pure milk of the word, that by it you may grow in respect to salvation, if you have tasted of the kindness of the Lord."* For a Christian the Bible is just as important as milk is for a baby. Normally, one would not think of going without physical food for a week or even a day. No matter what stage of life we are in—baby or adult—physical food is necessary for physical growth and health. Without food, one eventually becomes weak and may become ill. Lack of spiritual food has the same kind of effect on our spiritual lives.

 Consider your walk with God. Looking at the list below, mark all the different ways that you can study God's Word of which you are currently taking advantage.

___ sermons at church	___ Sunday school	___ books
___ discipleship classes	___ radio programs	___ tapes
___ television	___ personal study	___ CD's

While all of these are good, many of them can be of a passive nature if we aren't careful. We can listen to others without doing what the Berean Christians did. Not only did they receive Paul's teaching with eagerness, but they also examined the Scriptures for themselves to see whether or not those things were so. And they were willing to act on what they learned.

APPLY Rate yourself in each of these three important areas:

Hearing the Word

Not doing well ◄ 1 2 3 4 5 ► Doing well

Examining and Studying the Word

Not doing well ◄ 1 2 3 4 5 ► Doing well

Applying the Word to My Daily Life

Not doing well ◄ 1 2 3 4 5 ► Doing well

One thing that helps us be consistent in studying the Bible is to have a plan. This may involve working through a particular Bible study workbook like this one. Or it may involve systematically studying a book of the Bible on our own. You can learn much by taking only a chapter a day or even a paragraph a day and asking the four key questions of application we looked at in Day Four. Another way to study is to pick a topic and use a concordance, find different passages that speak about that topic. For example, if you want to learn about prayer, try looking up different passages where the word "prayer" or "pray" is used. Make sure you take time to look at the verse in its context. Another beneficial study is the character-based study. This involves picking a biblical personality and looking at all the different passages in Scripture that mention him or her. The **Following God**™ Bible character study series can help you learn more about prominent biblical characters and take you to the passages that teach about them. The **Following God**™ discipleship series covers difficult subjects ranging from how we should worship God to finding His will for our lives.

APPLY As you consider your Bible study plan, what are you going to do next after you finish this study?

___ Book of the Bible (write which book) _____

___ Bible Topic: _____

___ Bible Character: _____

___ Bible Study Workbook: _____

When will you do it?

_____

_____

_____

_____

Where will you do it?

_____

_____

_____

"I want to know one thing—if God Himself has condescended to teach the way. He hath written it down in a book. . . . Oh, give me that book! At any price, give me the book of God!"

—John Wesley

Another thing that helps us be consistent in studying the Bible is not just to have a plan, but also to have accountability. Are there others with whom you can study, or is there a trusted friend whom you can ask to hold you accountable and ask you how you are doing?

_____

_____

_____

I have found that being part of a Bible study group that meets once a week really helps me greatly. I study more and am more consistent when I have the encouragement and accountability of studying with others. If there isn't an option of such a study at your church, why not start one? You don't have to teach it, just facilitate it. You can help your group learn from each other as you study the Word of God together. God's Word always has effect. It will not return void without accomplishing its purpose, the prophet Isaiah told us. The apostle Paul in 1 Thessalonians 2:13 spoke of the Scriptures as that *"which also performs its work in you who believe."* God's Word works. It ministers wherever it is read and studied.

As you think about your relationship to the Word of God, why not close out this week's lesson by writing out a prayer, thanking God for all His Word is able to do in your life. You may want to review Psalm 19 and make it your own prayer in the space below.

_____

_____

_____

_____

_____

_____

_____

_____

_____

_____

_____

_____

_____

_____

_____

_____

_____

_____

Notes

Notes

step six

Personal Devotions

Imagine you have just met that perfect someone. That person is everything you have been looking for in a relationship. As you get to know that person, your love for him or her grows and you begin to see yourself spending the rest of your life with that person. What would you do to develop a good relationship with that special someone? Would you say, "Boy, it sure was good meeting you—I hope we see each other once in a while"? Probably not. If you were faced with such a relationship, you would not likely be so passive. You would not want time with that person to simply be left to chance. Instead, you would want to spend time with that person, getting to know him or her better. You would want to just enjoy being with that person, fellowshipping, making that person a priority. You would share with this person your deepest thoughts, wishes, desires, and everything going on in your life. Placing extreme importance on every word he or she has to say, you would want to communicate with and listen to that person—making sure you had time together. The things that we do to get to know someone are the same kinds of things we should do to get to know God. Look back over this paragraph and think about what we discussed from the vantage point of a relationship with God.

Just as a wedding ceremony isn't all there is to being married, becoming a Christian isn't all there is to a relationship with God.

To grow closer to God, we must spend time with Him.

It is only the beginning. To grow closer to God, we must spend time with Him. We must follow Him. Every believer is a disciple of Jesus Christ. The word "disciple" means "follower." Each Christian is either a good disciple (follower) or a bad one, but every true believer is a disciple. What one's goal ought to be is to keep growing in being a faithful follower, developing a more intimate relationship with God as a branch does with the vine. In John 15:7–8 we saw that the foundation of being God's disciples is that we abide in Him and His words abide in us. We looked at this principle of abiding in lessons 3 and 4. In the last lesson, we began looking at the importance of Scripture—His words abiding in us—and we will continue to build on that foundation in this lesson. From that foundation of abiding in Him and His words abiding in us, we move into a relationship with God in which we can ask what we wish and expect that He will do it. Next week we will look at the importance of prayer; but this week we want to focus on the bridge between the abiding aspects of our relationship with God, and prayer. It is what the saints of old often called a "quiet time" or personal devotions—spending time with God, listening to what He has to say, and talking with Him honestly from our hearts.

We looked last week at the principle of Bible study—and certainly we should study the Scriptures—but Bible study cannot be simply an intellectual pursuit of information. It should be the foundation of relationship. As we read and study the Word of God, we must at the same time be pursuing the God of the Word.

 *Personal Devotions* **DAY ONE**

Motivations for Time with God

The godless German philosopher, Nietzche, once made the statement, "If a man has a 'why?' in his life, he can overcome almost any 'how?'" While Nietzche is normally not a source of wisdom I would point you toward, he did make an astute observation about human nature in that comment. We need to know why we need to do something more than we need to know how. If we answer the "why?" question, we will have the motivation needed to keep seeking until we figure out how. If you study the teaching method of Jesus closely, you will find that He always answered the "why?" questions. He didn't want to simply give His disciples rules to follow—the Pharisees were good at doing that. Instead, He wanted His disciples to **think**, not just to **do.** As we look at the importance of personal devotions, it is important to begin by answering the "why?" question—"Why should we spend regular time alone with God?" Let's look at some of the reasons the Bible gives us. . . .

📖 Read 2 Peter 1:2–4. What reasons does Peter give us for getting to know God?

_____

_____

_____

_____

_____

What an awesome thought! Through knowing Him, God has given us everything we need for living a godly life. The more we get to know Him, the more success we will have in life and godliness. In verse 4, that idea is expanded to include not just knowing Him, but also knowing His precious and magnificent promises (the Scriptures). As a result of knowing Him and His Word, we get to partake of His nature, and escape the corruption of this fallen world. If we are Christians, we will spend eternity with God, but we don't have to wait until then to start getting to know Him.

📖 Look at John 15:15. What kind of relationship does Jesus want with His followers?

_____

_____

_____

_____

It may not sound very profound at first, but Jesus made a point of clarifying that He did not want to relate to His followers as slaves, but as friends. Obedience is important, but why do we obey? Is it only because we fear God's wrath if we don't obey? If so, we don't understand the Christian life as Jesus intended it. He wants our obedience to be a response of gratitude flowing out of our friendship with Him, not something we do to try and earn a relationship with Him. Taking the Ten Commandments and stretching them into 642 different laws and regulations, the Pharisees painted a harsh and legalistic portrait of God as needing to be appeased. Jesus did the opposite. He took the Ten Commandments and distilled them down to one—"Love God." In Matthew 22:37–40, Jesus said the whole law is fulfilled in the command to love God with all our heart, soul, and mind.

📖 Take some time to read through Lamentations 3:22–23 and then answer the questions that follow.

How does God feel toward us?

_____

_____

What do you think it means that they are *new every morning*?

_____

_____

_____

_____

What an encouragement to know that God's steadfast, loyal, covenant-keeping love toward us never ceases nor fails! And yet it is so easy to go through the day and never once remember God's great love for us. We can easily get caught up and entangled in the affairs of everyday life and rob ourselves of this great source of hope.

Perhaps the greatest truth held here is found in verse 23 in the little phrase *"they are new every morning."* I remember reading this verse one morning and suddenly being gripped with its sobering reality. If the Lord's loving

> **"No longer do I call you slaves, for the slave does not know what his master is doing; but I have called you friends, for all things that I have heard from My Father I have made known to you."**
>
> **—Jesus John 15:15**

> **"The LORD's loving-kindnesses indeed never cease, For His compassions never fail. They are new every morning; Great is Thy faithfulness."**
>
> **Lamentations 3:22–23**

kindnesses and compassions are new every morning and I let other commitments and choices squeeze out time with God on a given day, **then that is a part of God that I will never see this side of heaven**—a missed opportunity for growth, for encouragement, for hope, for grasping more fully the greatness of God's love.

We will spend eternity getting to know God, yet because of His love, He has made Himself known in a new way every day. But the choice is left with us. When we choose to meet with Him, we find Him. It is God's desire to meet with us—to disclose Himself to us. That alone ought to motivate us to want to spend time with Him each day.

MODELS OF TIME SPENT WITH GOD

Logic tells us that we need to spend time with God. But Scripture doesn't stop there. As we look at the people who have followed God, we discover the importance of personal devotions modeled over and over. We see in the lives of the saints as well as the Savior, the choice to carve out time to spend with God. One of the real benefits of Scripture is that it doesn't just tell us what to do, or even why to do it, but it also shows us how. The Bible is filled with personal accounts of lives that we can learn from. Today, we want to look at some of the models in Scripture of spending time with God.

If we want to know what it means to walk with God, we need to start with Jesus. God took on human frailties so He could show us the life and purpose for which He created us. In Jesus' humanity, we see a perfect model to follow of spending time with God, our Father.

📖 Look at Mark 1:35 and answer the questions that follow.

When did Jesus spend time with God, the Father?

_____

_____

Where did He go?

_____

_____

_____

Why do you think He left the house?

_____

_____

_____

This verse is brief, but speaks volumes about Jesus' priority of having time alone with His Father. Jesus got up while it was still dark. He sacrificed time; He took initiative. He went out into the wilderness, to a secluded place, intentionally leaving the house where He was staying. We find in the verses that follow that everyone was looking for Him and His disciples eventually found Him. Imagine how short His time with God the Father would have been if He had stayed at the house. He found a place free from distraction and interruption, where He could talk to His Father.

While the Gospel of Mark records this as an event, it is clear that it was not an isolated event. When Jesus went with His disciples to Gethsemane to pray, Luke uses the phrase, *"as was His custom"* to describe it (Luke 22:39). Morning was not the exclusive plan for Jesus spending time with God the Father. Matthew 14:23 says that after Jesus sent the crowds He had ministered to away, *"He went up on the mountain by Himself to pray; and when it was evening, He was there alone."* For Jesus, time with God was a priority, and He was flexible enough to adjust to the changing schedule of a busy life.

📖 Read these Psalms of David and write what you learn in them about his time with God.

Psalm 5:1–3

_____

_____

_____

_____

Psalm 63:1

_____

_____

_____

_____

Psalm 92:1–2

_____

_____

_____

_____

_____

"And in the early morning, while it was still dark, He arose and went out and departed to a lonely place, and was praying there."

Mark 1:35

David was called "a man after God's own heart" (see 1 Samuel 13:14; Acts 13:22). Over the course of his life, he developed a deeply intimate and personal relationship with God as reflected in the many psalms he wrote. In Psalm 5, we see that he talked with God in the morning, but also that he listened and awaited God's reply—his habit was to *"eagerly watch."* In Psalm 63:1, we see that he sought God *"earnestly."* Psalm 92 indicates that David's time with God included thankfulness and praise for God's loving kindness and faithfulness. Also, we see there that he did this both in the morning and at night. These would seem to be the most logical times to meet with God, either at the beginning of our day or at the end of it.

📖 Another model we find in Scripture of one who met with God is Moses. Look at Exodus 33:7–11 and record what you learn there.

_____

_____

_____

Moses used to pitch a tent a good distance outside the camp as a place for people to meet with God. It is interesting that this principle of a quiet place, free from distraction, was observed all the way back to Moses' day. God would speak to Moses in that tent of meeting. The pillar of cloud, a visible manifestation of God's presence, would hover over that tent; and when the people saw that cloud, they would worship (verse 10). When we practice the principle of personal devotions, we have something Moses and Israel did not have. We have the written word of God through which He will speak to us. Yet the principle of meeting with God remains the same.

THE METHODS OF PERSONAL DEVOTIONS

What is the right way to spend time with God? Think about that question before you answer. Think about the parallel to human relationships. Is there a list somewhere of all the things you have to do on a date? Is time with someone you love something that can be regimented or rattled off like a checklist? We must remind ourselves that personal devotions are not the goal—they are a means to the goal. The real objective is to develop a love relationship with the Lord. We can check each item off our list and miss the whole point. A quiet time is not a task to accomplish, but a time to pursue our relationship with God. There is no absolute right or wrong way to do it. There is no magical time limit or minimum frequency. We must be careful to focus on the principle of **time with God** instead of the **program** of personal devotions.

When we consider the kinds of things that ought to be a part of spending time with God, we have already observed a number of principles in the passages we have looked at so far. We saw from the examples of Jesus and Moses the importance of finding a place free from distraction where we can be quiet and focus on the Lord. In David, we saw the importance of timing. Generally speaking, for most of us either first thing in the morning or at night before bed will be the best times to meet with God. But that really depends on you, your temperament, and life demands. For a mother with small children, during the children's nap may be the best time for personal devotions. For some with variable work schedules, during lunch break may be better. Many of the saints of old made it their habit in the early morning hours. I tried the wee hours of the morning, but often my quiet time got a little too quiet. My best hours are at night. I used to think that morning was more spiritual until I realized that before electricity, daylight was a necessary ingredient. God doesn't tell us when, and I think that is significant. We have freedom to be who we are.

What is the main purpose of time with God? For one thing, it is not to earn God's favor or avoid His wrath. He loves us unconditionally. He doesn't love us more when we have a quiet time, and He doesn't love us less if we don't. The real purpose of personal devotions is to know God more and to enjoy our relationship with Him. We need to be taught by Him, and to become like Him. We need to keep Him as priority in our hearts. That takes time.

The contents of quality time with God, simply put, are prayer and the Word—talking with God and hearing from God. But when we speak of prayer, we must be specific in what we mean. Prayer is asking God to do things, but it is much more than that. True prayer is more than spouting off to the Lord a grocery list of requests. Prayer also includes adoration, confession, and thanksgiving. One thing that has helped me to organize my prayer time is the helpful acrostic, A.C.T.S. **"A"** stands for adoration, and that is where I start—focusing on God, not me. **"C"** is for confession. I think that the order here is important. If I start with confession, my focus is on me. I will see as much of my sin as I need to see when my eyes are on the Lord. Adoration starts me out at the right place. Confession is a response to conviction, God's work. **"T"** stands for thanksgiving, and **"S"** stands for supplication (requests). Again, the order is important. Thanksgiving should come before supplication, for I need to be reminded of all God has already done, before asking Him to do something. These four types of prayer make up my normal time with Him. Let's look at some Scriptural examples of each.

ADORATION

📖 Look at the verses below and write what you see in them of adoration of God.

Psalm 145:1–2

_____

_____

_____

Psalm 29:1–2

_____

_____

_____

In Psalm 145, David writes, *"I will extol you, my God."* To "extol" means to lift up, or exalt. When we "extol" the Lord, we hold His attributes up, reminding ourselves of who He is. It includes "blessing" and "praising" Him. David said in verse 2, He would do this *"every day."* In Psalm 29, we see that we are to "ascribe to the LORD" the glory that is due Him. Adoration really involves just focusing in on who God is, not so much what He does. (Focusing on what God does falls under thanksgiving.)

CONFESSION

📖 Read these verses and write what you learn from them about confession.

Psalm 139:23–24

_____

_____

_____

Prayer
PRAYER GUIDELINES

A good guide for time in prayer is the acrostic, ACTS.

A—Adoration, worshipping God for who He is—His attributes and character

C—Confession, agreeing with God about our sins

T—Thanksgiving, worshiping and praising God for what He does

S—Supplication, bringing our requests to God

_____

_____

_____

Here in Psalm 139, we see one of the reasons why David could be called "a man after God's own heart." He was willing to let God convict him of his sins. Notice that he didn't try to deal with his sin himself, nor did he even try to find sin in his heart. Instead, he invited God to shine the searchlight of His Holy Spirit into the dark corners to find any dirt that needed to be dealt with. King David serves as a good model of how to keep a clean heart. If we desire to live lives that are pleasing to God, it is essential that we open our hearts to Him and let Him cleanse them. Remember though, it is God's job to find the sin, not ours. Often Satan sneaks us into the trap of intro-spection—looking for sin in everything we do. If he cannot tempt us into sin, then he will try to discourage us by causing us to focus on ourselves looking for sin in every attitude and action. The result is condemnation, dis-couragement and frustration. Satan robs us of our joy by saddling us with the responsibilities of judging our own hearts. Realize however, that this is an impossible task. Jeremiah lamented, "*the heart is more deceitful than all else and is desperately sick;* **who can understand it?**" (Jeremiah 17:9). In other words, if we try to search our own hearts, we will fail. Either we will find sin where there is none, resulting in enslavement to legalism, or we will jus-tify away our sin, resulting in further license. Only God can judge our hearts accurately. David shows us how this can happen—by calling on the Lord to search our hearts. If we sincerely desire to please the Lord, we can be confi-dent that as we seek Him, His Holy Spirit who indwells us will reveal any sin that stands in the way of fellowship with the Father. This revealing is what David prays for in Psalm 26:2. He asks God to examine his heart.

ONLY GOD CAN ACCURATELY JUDGE HEARTS

"The heart is more deceitful than all else and is desperately sick; who can under-stand it? I, the LORD, search the heart, I test the mind, Even to give to each man according to his ways, according to the results of his deeds." (Jeremiah 17:9–10)

THANKSGIVING

📖 Consider Psalm 30:1–4 and write what you see of the psalmist's thanks-giving.

_____

_____

_____

In this psalm, David thanks God for what He has personally done for him, particularly for granting him protection and deliverance from his enemies and for healing him. In this case, it seems David is grateful to God for eas-ing his mind from fear and discouragement and simply for keeping him alive. We need to take time to thank God for all He does for us. Not only does it help us to be grateful, but it also helps our faith. As we remember what God has already done, it helps us trust Him more.

SUPPLICATION

📖 What do you learn in Philippians 4:6 that we are to do with our worries and cares?

_____

_____

_____

I love the way the New Living Translation (NLT) translates this verse. It says simply, *"Don't worry about anything; instead, pray about everything."* God wants us to bring our requests to Him. We'll delve more into the concept of prayer in the next lesson, but remember, God welcomes our requests.

THE MEANS OF HEARING FROM GOD

As we consider the content of time with God, we have already seen the importance of the Word. God's Word is His communication with us. We long for God to speak to us, and yet, He already has. Often it will happen that by reading the Bible, the Spirit of God will personalize some verse to us and speak directly to our situation. Hebrews 4:12 says, *"The word of God is living and active and sharper than any two-edged sword, and piercing as far as the division of soul and spirit, of both joints and marrow, and able to judge the thoughts and intentions of the heart."* The Bible is no ordinary book! As we spend time with God, He speaks to our hearts and most of what He says, He says through the Bible. Today we want to talk about the ingredients of a meaningful time with God.

📖 Read Psalm 1:1–3 and write what you learn about the habit of the godly man.

_____

_____

_____

The obvious point to be seen here is that the godly man meditates on the Word of God *"day and night,"* and as a result, he prospers. The less obvious point is how crucial this meditation is to helping us avoid walking *"in the counsel of the wicked."* How do we recognize what is wrong counsel apart from studying that which is right? A regular diet of meditating on the Word of God is essential to becoming godly. The word, "meditate" (not to be confused with the New Age term) has nothing to do with "emptying your mind," but rather has the idea of filling your mind with God's truth and thinking about it continually. We need to meditate as we read.

📖 Take a look at Psalm 15:1–2 and record what you see.

_____

_____

_____

_____

One of the ingredients of a meaningful relationship with God is a pure heart. A pure heart is not some mystical gift, but the result of dealing with things as we go through life. Often as we are spending time with God, He will put His finger on something in our hearts that needs to be confronted and addressed. Matthew 5:8 says, *"Blessed are the pure in heart, for they shall see God."* Our willingness to deal with our hearts truthfully moves us toward a purer heart, resulting in a greater vision of God.

Word Study
MEDITATE

The Old Testament (Hebrew) word for meditate in Psalm 1:2 is *Haghah,* and literally means, "to murmur or mutter." It is possible that the Scriptures were read audibly during the process of meditation. The idea of the word meant "to muse." The New Testament (Greek) term for meditate is *meletao,* and means, to ponder over something. The idea is much like the English word, "ruminate"—the practice of farm animals "chewing their cud." Just as a cow chews and rechews the grass until it is digested, we should chew and rechew the verses until we have digested their meaning.

📖 Read Psalm 66:18. What happens to my quiet time if I do not deal with sin in my heart?

_____

_____

_____

_____

_____

If I sin in my heart and am not willing to deal with it, it will begin to cloud my fellowship with God. We need to be quick to deal with sin as God reveals it. It is my keeping of a pure heart that enables me to see Him.

📖 What do we find in Matthew 5:23–24 that affects the practice of spending time with God?

_____

_____

_____

_____

_____

Jesus makes an important point here—our relationships with others affect our relationship with God. Think about how this impacts spending time with God. Sometimes the most important thing that comes out of spending time with God is going to a brother to mend a relationship. Our unwillingness to make things right with our brothers may keep us from having fellowship with God.

You cannot be changed by one experience into spiritual maturity any more than you can become a full-grown adult by eating one meal.

FOR ME TO FOLLOW GOD

We have looked at many different principles about personal devotions. What is the most important one? It is this: what you do when you spend time with God is not nearly so important as **that** you spend time with God. Spiritual growth is not the result of a dramatic experience, but the result of a lot of small steps. You cannot be changed by one experience into spiritual maturity any more than you can become a full-grown adult by eating one meal. You will eat many meals in your lifetime, and probably they won't all be identical. Each will satisfy in its own way, but you will hunger again. Think of spending time with God as one meal in the whole plan of your Spiritual nutrition. If you are doing something that isn't satisfying your spiritual hunger, then change your diet. But whatever you do—don't give up eating.

 An important thing to consider as we look at the importance of personal devotions is asking the question, "What might keep me from spending time with God?" Consider the possibilities on the next page, and check the three that have the greatest potential of getting in the way of consistently spending time with God.

___ Don't know what to do   ___ Lack of a place   ___ Not a priority

___ Changing work schedule   ___ Boredom   ___ Sin in my life

___ Don't see the importance   ___ Too busy   ___ Not organized

___ Not planning ahead   ___ Other _____

Habits are easier to form if we can be consistent. If you can plan to spend time with God the same time every day, it may be easier. But even if you can't, you can still build the habit. It comes down to planning and choice. If you think you don't have time for personal devotions, it may be that you have unrealistic expectations. Maybe you think that if you cannot spend a whole hour in a quiet time, then you have failed. Perhaps your goal should be something more realistic. Make it your aim to spend at least five minutes a day with God. What you will discover is that on those days when that is all you can do, you will not be discouraged by feelings of guilt. But you will also find that those five minutes will create a desire for more time with God, and you will make that time as you can.

To make time with God a habit is hard without a plan. You don't want to start each time trying to decide what to do each day. There are many tools that can help you with personal devotions. Let me suggest a few that have been meaningful to me.

- ✓ In months with thirty days, I like to read every thirtieth Psalm based on what day of the month it is. For example, if it is the fifth of the month, I read Psalms 5, 35, 65, 95, and 125.

- ✓ Read a chapter of Proverbs. There are thirty-one chapters—this works good with months of thirty-one days.

- ✓ Work through a book of the Bible. Perhaps you can read one to two chapters per day of a particular book.

- ✓ A good devotional book. There are a great many devotional books written to help you spend time with God. My favorite is *My Utmost for His Highest* by Oswald Chambers. It is a classic.

- ✓ Read through the Bible in a year.

The key is not to pick one and feel that is all you can ever do. Vary your time. Be creative in developing your relationship with God. Write prayers to God. Play praise music and sing to the Lord. Go for a walk, praying over your concerns as you go. Keep a spiritual diary, writing your thoughts and struggles. Make sure to allow time for meditation, rather than just piling up information. Whatever I am doing in the Word, I like to read until I sense God speaking to me in a personal way from a verse or verses. Then I will stop there and reread, meditating on what it says. Often that is a springboard to prayer as I talk to God about what the passage is saying to me. Since my main goal is to spend time with God, not just to check personal devotions off my to-do list, I don't worry if I don't finish. I just pick up my reading next time wherever I left off.

I usually begin my time in a brief prayer, asking God to speak to me today. Then I read the Word with whatever plan I am using at the time (I change plans regularly for variety—that works best for me). Journaling helps me to remember what I learn—writing out in a notebook the main thought I saw in the Word, and one or more applications to me personally.

Extra Mile
QUIET TIME

Some "Quiet Time" ideas...

- Read every thirtieth Psalm
- Read a chapter of Proverbs
- Work through a book of the Bible
- Buy a devotional book
- Plan to read the Bible in a year

After reading and meditating on the Word, I spend time in prayer, using the ACTS acrostic to guide me (**A**doration, **C**onfession, **T**hanksgiving, **S**upplication). When I get to supplication, I split that time between praying for needs and burdens on my heart, and praying for people that are important to me. As a general rule, if anything is significant enough to worry about, it is important to pray about. As for people, I pray for family, friends, missionaries, unsaved that I know, governmental authorities, spiritual leaders, etc. I've never run out of people to pray for. It may be helpful if you assign a different theme for each day of the week—pray for one or two of those groups each day (e.g., on Sunday pray for spiritual leaders, Monday for co-workers, Tuesday for friends, Wednesday for missionaries, Thursday for the unsaved, Friday for governmental authorities, Saturday for family).

 If the principle of personal devotions is to become a regular habit, you need to have a plan. When you aim at nothing, you are sure to hit it every time. Fill out your plan in the space below.

When? When are you going to spend time with the Lord?

_____

_____

_____

What? What are you going to use for a plan? Consider the list above for some ideas.

_____

_____

_____

_____

Where? Where can you have your quiet time that will be free from interruption and distraction?

_____

_____

_____

_____

Who? Whom will you pray for?

_____

_____

_____

_____

Taking time to plan is key. But if your time alone with God is to become a habit, you must also have a backup or contingency plan in place for when things go awry. If you miss a day, don't get discouraged. Satan would love for you to give up. We think he wins if we miss a day, but really he wins only if missing a day makes us miss another. If your quiet time starts getting dry, be sure and build in some variety. Change things around. Don't let yourself get stuck in a rut, but at the same time, don't judge the quality of your time

Satan would love for you to give up. We think he wins if we miss a day, but really he wins only if missing a day makes us miss another.

with God by emotions. If you have talked to God, if you have learned something from His Word, you should see that as progress.

The most important principle is to make a decision. To not decide is to decide not to do it. Why not make a commitment for the next month to spend time with God every day.

Any deepening love relationship requires spending time together, and a relationship with God is no different. David wrote, *"in the morning I will order my prayer to Thee and eagerly watch"* (Psalm 5:3). Prayerfully consider this commitment to God and formalize it by signing your name.

 "Lord, I commit to faithfully spend time with you every day for the next two weeks, and to meet with you with a whole heart. I ask you to speak to me what I need to hear, and to convict me of anything in my heart and life that would hinder my walking with you."

SIGNED _____

Why not write your own prayer of application to the Lord in the space below.

_____
_____
_____
_____
_____
_____
_____
_____
_____
_____
_____
_____
_____
_____
_____
_____
_____
_____
_____
_____
_____
_____
_____

Notes

step seven

Prayer

The office of President of the United States is without a doubt unparalleled in its strategic importance upon world affairs. The President of the United States is perhaps the most influential person in the world. During the difficult days of the "Cold War" when the greatest adversary of the U.S. was the Soviet Union, the President had access to a "hotline" to the Kremlin, a direct phone line that allowed him immediate access to the Soviet premier. This communication was set up so that difficulties could be worked out quickly in hopes that war could be averted between the two great countries. What would it be like if you had such a hotline to the President? Imagine having the ability (and the freedom) to call him any time night or day. That would be a tremendous privilege. You would likely place great value upon such lofty access and use it sparingly and respectfully. You would not want to take too much of the President's time, or waste the privilege on trivial matters. Yet that concern would be very different if you were not just any citizen, but a child of the President. Then you would feel much freer to make use of access privileges.

The Christian has a far greater hotline—not to the President of the United States, but to the Creator of the universe. Each child of God has direct access to Him through prayer, and God invites

"Call to me, and I will answer you, and I will tell you great and mighty things, which you do not know."

Jeremiah 33:3

His children to use this hotline regularly. He is not imposed upon when we contact Him, nor is His schedule interrupted. We don't need to worry about whether the topic of conversation is too trivial or of no interest to Him. Because He loves us, He values whatever is important to us. Because He desires a relationship with us, He welcomes our conversation. Jeremiah 33:3 says, *"Call to Me, and I will answer you, and I will tell you great and mighty things, which you do not know."* Our person-to-person call will always be accepted. In this lesson, we want to focus on the privilege of prayer and how we can make use of this wonderful part of our relationship with God.

Prayer **DAY ONE**

THE OPPORTUNITY OF PRAYER

It is amazing how easily we forget to pray. We often forget what a resource God is for our decisions and discussions. In Hebrews 10:19–22 we see the Old Testament High Priest coming into the presence of God contrasted with how the believer accesses God's presence today. Once a year, the High Priest went into the Holy of Holies, offering to God the blood of a bull. This blood could not take away sin, but could only temporarily atone for it. How different it is for us today!

📖 Read Hebrews 10:19–22.

How is our entering of the Holy Place in the Church Age different than the experience of the priest?

_____

_____

_____

_____

What is it that allows us into God's presence?

_____

_____

_____

What should our response be to this priviledge (verse 22)?

_____

_____

_____

God's presence is always open to us. In the Old Testament times the priest entered the Holy of Holies (God's presence) only once a year in fear and trembling. This day is called *Yom Kippur* or the "Day of Atonement." This privilege was open **only** to the High Priest, and **only** on that day. Today we can enter into God's presence at any time, with confidence, through the blood of Christ (Hebrews 10:19). His perfect sacrifice makes us acceptable to be in God's presence. Yet most believers rarely exercise this incredible privilege. *"Let us draw near. . . ."* the writer of Hebrews tells us.

Did You Know?

❓ **"YOM KIPPUR"**

The High Priest was allowed past the veil of the temple only once a year on *Yom Kippur*, the Day of Atonement. He would enter into the Holy of Holies to sprinkle sacrificial blood on the mercy seat to atone for the sins of the nation. While he was inside, the nation would wait in silence. When he went inside, a rope would be tied to his ankle, for if his sacrifice was not acceptable, he would die in the presence of the Lord, and no one could go inside to retrieve the body. The hem of his robe was strung with bells, and the attendants could hear him moving around. This was their reassurance that he was still alive. When he came outside, the nation would cheer, for this was the proof that their sins were atoned.

But what if we draw near in a wrong way? What if our attitude is wrong? Will God still hear our prayers then? I think if each of us is honest we would have to admit that sometimes we don't come to the Lord in prayer—either because we do not feel worthy, or we do not think He hears us due to our attitudes.

📖 Look at Psalm 55:17 and write what you learn about the types of prayers God will hear.

_____

_____

_____

_____

What an amazing verse! It is incredible to think that because God is my heavenly Father, He hears all that I say. Even when my prayers are filled with complaining and murmuring, He still hears them. When we understand the reality of Hebrews 10—that we have access to the presence of God with confidence through the blood of Jesus—then we can begin to comprehend that it is not our worthiness that causes God to hear our prayers but the worthiness of Christ. That is why we pray in Jesus' name instead of in our own name. Our access is not based on our worthiness, but His.

📖 Look at the verses below in light of what you have seen, and write what you learn about how God views your prayers.

Proverbs 15:8

_____

_____

_____

_____

Proverbs 15:29

_____

_____

_____

_____

In Proverbs 15:8, we see that the _"prayer of the upright"_ is His delight. In other words, God takes delight in hearing what we have to say to Him. Just as a proud father cherises the simple words of a toddler, it is not flowery words or proper language that makes God turn His ear to us, but His parental love. Proverbs 15:29 echoes this idea, affirming that He hears the prayers of the righteous—in other words, the prayers of those with a right relationship to Him.

As someone once said, "There is a lot you can do once you have prayed, but you can do nothing until you pray." If we run about trying to solve problems without first listening to God, we will be following ourselves like a dog chasing its own tail, and we will get nowhere. But clearly, God has granted us the opportunity to pray.

> *"The prayer of the upright is His delight."*
> **Proverbs 15:8**

THE FUNDAMENTALS OF PRAYER

Everyone of us has had different experiences in prayer. Some of you may have cut your spiritual teeth on "Now I lay me down to sleep. . . ." Others may feel very inadequate and uncomfortable in prayer. Still others may perceive prayer as a ritual: kneeling and/or bowing the head, folding the hands, reciting a grocery list of requests interspersed with sixteenth-century English, perhaps out of reverence for God or perhaps because we believe that is how God talks. Yet most of us really don't understand prayer as a fundamental part of a relationship with God.

Certain aspects of our faith are fundamental, things we never outgrow. We apply these things every day regardless of how mature we are in Christ. Prayer is one such fundamental. I am reminded of the great football coach, Vince Lombardi, who started the first practice of every season with the same line: "This is a football." His message was loud and clear—success isn't found in the flashy stuff, but in the fundamentals. The same is true in our spiritual lives.

The first fundamental of prayer is that it is simply communicating with God from our hearts. Because of this, there is no such thing as an insincere prayer. If it isn't from our hearts, it isn't prayer, even if we call it that. It is only "lip-service" or religious ritual. Like me, you may have listened to other people pray and wondered if any of the words even made it past the ceiling.

Unfortunately, many prayers offered in public gatherings are merely sermonettes to each other. Sadly, we worry so much about wording our prayer the right way that we forget we are talking to God. We fail to realize God isn't concerned about the wording as much as He is about our attitude. So the first fundamental of prayer: **it must be honest communication from our heart to the heart of God.**

📖 Read Matthew 6:5.

What does Jesus call the person who prays outloud in order to be heard by those around him?

_____

_____

What is the outcome of such praying?

_____

_____

_____

> **True prayer is powerful only because God is powerful.**

The one who prays with a view to being heard by those around him, Jesus calls a hypocrite. When we pray to be noticed by others, Jesus makes it clear that the only reward we will have is that we are noticed by others. We are not noticed by God.

The second fundamental of prayer is that, contrary to the teachings of many, **there is no power in the prayer itself.** Before you start tying me to the stake and piling up the brush, let me explain. Often we profess and promote the erroneous idea that prayer has some intrinsic power in itself. In doing so, we place our faith in prayer instead of the God we pray to. This doctrine derives more from Eastern mysticism and the New Age movement than from biblical Christianity. True prayer is powerful only because God is powerful. *The real power of prayer is our connection with the all-powerful Creator.* Prayer is not a means of twisting God's arm, but of communicating with Him openly.

📖 Read Matthew 6:7.

What do the Gentiles (unbelievers in this case) trust to be heard by God?

_____

_____

_____

_____

Pagans wrongly think that there is some mystical power in spoken words. They think if the prayer is long enough or wordy enough, somehow its length and wordiness will make it more acceptable to any deities that might happen to be listening. But clearly, they are wrong. Jesus says, *"do not use meaningless repetition, as the Gentiles do."* There is no power in the act of praying, only in the One we pray to.

The third fundamental of prayer is: **nothing is off-limits.** We can (and should) pray about anything and everything.

📖 Read 1 Peter 5:7. What does it say about prayer?

_____

_____

_____

Peter exhorts us to "cast all our cares" on God. If anything is significant enough for us to worry about it, then it is significant enough to pray about it. The operative word here is **ALL**. We can cast all our anxieties on the Lord. We do this through prayer. Nothing is too trivial to bring to the Lord.

Put Yourself In Their Shoes

JESUS' LESSONS ON PRAYER

Some lessons on prayer from the Sermon on the Mount (Matthew 6):

- Jesus said, "<u>When</u> you pray…" not "<u>IF</u> you pray"

- Jesus said, "Don't pray like a hypocrite"—talking to men instead of talking to God

- Jesus said, "Don't pray like a Gentile (unbeliever)"—trusting your words instead of trusting God.

THE PRACTICE OF PRAYER

Prayer DAY THREE

I have to be very careful how I explain the title of today's study. When I speak of "the Practice of Prayer," I do not mean it like the "practice" of medicine. It is not an activity reserved for the professionals. I just mean the actual "doing" of it. Any child of God can talk to his or her father. You don't have to speak King James English to talk with God. But at the same time, it is helpful if we understand how God wants us to talk with Him. A great passage to educate us on the proper practice of prayer is Philippians 4:6—*"Be anxious for nothing, but in everything by prayer and supplication with thanksgiving, let your requests be made known to God."* Here we find specific directions on how to proceed in prayer.

Look at each phrase in Philippians 4:6 and write your thoughts in the space provided.

"Be anxious for nothing. . ."

_____

_____

_____

". . . but in everything. . ."

_____

_____

_____

". . . by prayer and supplication. . ."

_____

_____

_____

". . . with thanksgiving. . ."

_____

_____

_____

". . . let your requests be made known to God."

_____

_____

_____

First, we must **choose to lay aside our anxiety.** Anxiety should always be viewed as a red flag, alerting us to the need to pray. Anxiety or worry can be a direct result of my trusting in myself and my own resources instead of in God. There are no guarantees that I will never be anxious, but if I let anxiety dictate my response to God, anxiety then becomes sin, and it should be dealt with as such. Next, the boundaries of prayer are given: **in everything.** No matter how much we weasel and squirm, we cannot escape the reality that God wants us to talk with Him about everything, every area of our lives. Anything less is disobedience. The third step in our process of prayer is **to pray.** This may sound silly, but the passage gives us specifics on how to go about this. First, Paul says, *"in everything by* **prayer."** These words relate to the means of general prayer directed to God. Next he says, *"and* **supplication."** The word "supplication" can best be described as petitioning for particular benefits, in other words, we are to make our requests specific. Next, we are told to accompany our requests with *"thanksgiving."* When we lay aside anxiety and pray for everything in an attitude of thanksgiving, we can make any request of God we desire. Sound too good to be true? No, it is simply God's invitation to honesty. He wants us to bare our hearts to Him.

Do I really want God to answer all my prayers, even if He knows that some of my requests are not in my best interests?

If we pray the right way, will God always give us what we ask for? Look at Philippians 4:7 and write what that verse teaches us.

_____

_____

_____

_____

Philippians 4:6 invites us to bring every request to God. We must notice, however, that there is no promise God will give us our every request. Sound unfair? Actually, what God promises is even better. Instead of promising to honor our request, regardless of whether it is beneficial to us or not, God promises to guard our hearts with His peace (Philippians 4:7). How does He do that? When we follow the specific formula of Philippians 4:6–7, we are, in essence, laying our request at God's feet. Once we've done that, we can have confidence that He hears us (Psalm 4:3). We can know that if our request is within His will, He'll give it to us. If not, He'll say no. Either way, we can have peace, because our request has now been filtered through God's will for us, which is *"good and acceptable and perfect"* (Romans 12:2).

But what if God's will is not what I want? Ask yourself this: "Do I really want what my all-loving, all-knowing heavenly Father says is not the best for me?" Are you willing to settle for something less than God's will?

The famous Christian author, C. S. Lewis, addressed the issue of answered prayer in a British newspaper article entitled "Work and Prayer" in 1945. This article was reprinted in Lewis's book, *God In The Dock* (copyright 1970 by C.S. Lewis Pte. Ltd., p.33), and a portion of that article appears below:

> The two methods by which we are allowed to produce events may be called work and prayer. . . . The kind of causality we exercise by work is, so to speak, divinely guaranteed, and therefore ruthless. By it we are free to do ourselves as much harm as we please. But the kind which we exercise by prayer is not like that; God has left Himself a discretionary power. Had He not done so, prayer would be an activity too dangerous for man. . . .
>
> Prayers are not always—in the crude, factual sense of the word—"granted." This is not because prayer is a weaker kind of causality, but because it is a stronger kind. When it 'works' at all it works unlimited by space and time. That is why God has retained a discretionary power of granting or refusing it; except on that condition, prayer would destroy us. It is not unreasonable for a headmaster to say, "Such and such things you may do according to the fixed rules of this school. But such and such other things are too dangerous to be left to general rules. If you want to do them you must come and make a request and talk over the whole matter with me in my study. And then—we'll see."

BARRIERS TO EFFECTIVE PRAYER

Prayer

While we are looking at this principle of prayer and how we ought to pray, we need to also ask the question, "What gets in the way of effective prayer?" For one thing, the most ineffective prayers are the ones that are never uttered. Just by talking to God, we are a step ahead. One near-fatal flaw we human beings have is our innate tendency to "lean on our own understanding." It is our trusting that we have all the answers that sometimes gets in the way of our praying. I'm not saying a Christian should unplug his brain, but the admonition of Proverbs 3:5, 6 makes it clear that limited, finite, human reasoning isn't adequate for all the decisions we are called to make. Instead we need to talk to God about things.

  Read Proverbs 3:5–6 and answer the following questions:

What is being contrasted with trusting the Lord in these verses?

_____

_____

_____

What do you think it means to "lean" on your own understanding?

_____

_____

_____

How do we *acknowledge Him* in all our ways?

_____

_____

_____

What is the result?

_____

_____

_____

Word Study
PROVERBS 3:5–6

Sha'an ("lean")—to lean against, to cause to support oneself. This verb depicts an attitude of trust.

Yadha' ("acknowledge")—to perceive, to understand, to acquire knowledge, to be familiar with, to be aware of.

'Orach ("paths")—this noun is normally translated "way" or "path." Most often it is used figuratively.

Yashar ("straight")—to be level, to make straight, to declare right. This word has two main meanings: literally (straight), and ethically (upright and moral).

Here in Proverbs 3 we see trusting the Lord contrasted with leaning on or trusting our own understanding. The Hebrew word for "lean" means "to support oneself." It doesn't mean that we don't use our own understanding; rather, it says that human logic alone is not sufficient to support us. The admonition to acknowledge Him in all our ways makes it clear that in every situation life brings our way, there is a need to bring that situation to the Lord through prayer. We must lean on the Lord and ask His wisdom in all our decisions. Then He will direct our paths. Perhaps the biggest mistake we can make is to trust ourselves so much that we don't pray at all. In the Sermon on the Mount Jesus said, "**When** *you pray. . .*" not "**If** *you pray.*"

  Another potential barrier to effective prayer is found in James 4:2. Read this verse and write what you learn.

_____

_____

_____

_____

The potential problem James mentions is that we do not have because we do not ask. Striving to get what we want in our own way instead of looking to God, we often simply try to figure out our own solutions instead of asking God for His. You may be saying, "But I have asked, and I still don't have." Let's analyze. In light of our fundamentals of true prayer, did your request really connect your faith to God, or did you place your faith in prayer? The difference is subtle but significant.

📖 Now look at James 4:3 and identify the barrier it gives.

_____

_____

_____

_____

Another barrier James mentions is that we do ask, but we ask with wrong motives. We don't really want what God wants for us, we only want our own pleasure—physical or emotional pleasure—the pleasure of a trial-free, work-free existence. In any case, this wrong motive gets in the way of Christ being Lord of our lives. It is a commitment to our will instead of God's.

In James 1:5 we find an incredible promise. He writes, *"If any of you lacks wisdom, let him ask of God, who gives to all men generously and without reproach, and it will be given to him."* We must, in faith, ask God for wisdom and guidance; and when we do, He fulfills His promise. Anyone who lacks wisdom or understanding is invited to ask God, and the promise is that He will give it to all. God's giving of wisdom when asked for is not done begrudgingly or sparingly, but generously and without reproach.
However, we cannot expect God to give us the wisdom we lack if we haven't even asked Him for it. Once we do, we can begin looking for His answer. But there is a potential problem revealed here as well.

📖 Read James 1:6. What gets in the way of answered prayer when we ask God for direction?

_____

_____

_____

_____

When we ask God for direction, we must look to Him to answer that request. We must exercise faith—we must trust that He will answer and be looking to Him for that answer. It is not that we must build up to a certain measure of faith—the proper amount. Jesus told His disciples if they had faith the size of a mustard seed, they could command a mountain to be cast into the sea and it would be done (see Matthew 17:20). It is not the amount of faith that is important, but that our faith is rooted in the right place. We must look to God to answer us, not simply throw a prayer toward heaven for good luck and then go our own way trying to figure things out on our own without looking to God for guidance. If we ask God to speak, how will He answer? By His Word and His Spirit. If we are asking in faith, we should be looking in the Bible for the answer and making time to be quiet before Him.

"You do not have because you do not ask. You ask and do not receive, because you ask with wrong motives, so that you may spend it on your pleasures."

James 4:2–3

"But let him ask in faith. . . ."

James 1:6

FOR ME TO FOLLOW GOD

One of the surest ways to guarantee a small crowd at church is to call a prayer meeting. People will be staying away in droves. Why is that? Why do we find it easier to do everything else in the Christian life besides prayer? First, I believe one of the things that keeps us from prayer is the fact that it is work. It requires focus to talk to God instead of talking to ourselves or those around us. Second, I think prayer is difficult because we expect it to be. We have been conditioned to dread prayer because of religious activities that were mere ritual. I am amazed at how people seem to enjoy a message that makes them feel bad about their prayer life. It is not so much that they expect anything to change as it is that they assume everyone else has a better prayer life than they have—yet they have no hope that their prayer life will ever change for the better. The next best thing, in their minds, to a good prayer life is at least feeling bad about not having one. But prayer shouldn't be that way. It is an opportunity and a privilege, not a burden. We just need to be able to separate it from the religious rituals that masquerade for true prayer.

 As you seek to apply these important principles of prayer, it is important to first evaluate where you are. Look at the list below and check the areas where you feel are struggling.

____ I'm so used to doing things myself, that I don't remember to talk to God about any issue.

____ I don't really see the need to pray.

____ I'm not sure that God really listens.

____ I don't feel worthy.

____ It hasn't seemed to work in the past.

____ I forget.

____ I lean too much on my own understanding (Prov. 3:5).

____ I tend to pray selfishly instead of in surrendered fashion.

____ Instead of laying aside all anxieties, I worry.

In light of what we have studied this week, where do you feel you need the most improvement?

_____

_____

_____

_____

When circumstances arise, how often do you pray about them before doing anything else?

Never_____

Rarely_____

Sometimes_____

Often_____

Always_____

APPLY We identified some specific steps to follow in praying as noted in Philippians 4:6–7

- ☑ I must choose to lay aside my anxiety.
- ☑ I must transfer my trust from myself to God.
- ☑ I must openly discuss every area with God.
- ☑ I must direct my prayer to Him in a specific manner and accompany it with thanksgiving.
- ☑ I may then bring **any** request to Him.
- ☑ I must trust Him for His peace and accept His answer, whatever it is.

Prayer

The best way to learn to pray is by praying. Bill Bright, the founder of Campus Crusade for Christ, defines prayer this way: "Prayer is simply talking to God. He is not so concerned with the words you use, as He is the attitude of your heart." Take a few minutes now to express your heart, writing to the Lord in the spaces provided below. Use the outline of Philippians 4:6–7 to guide you.

Lay aside anxiety…

_____

_____

_____

_____

_____

Openly discuss every area in a specific manner…

_____

_____

_____

_____

_____

Accompany it with thanksgiving…

_____

_____

_____

_____

_____

Bring your <u>request</u> (what <u>you</u> desire—be as specific as possible)…

_____

_____

_____

_____

_____

> "Prayer is simply talking to God. He is not so concerned with the words you use, as He is the attitude of your heart."
>
> **—Bill Bright**
> *Founder and Chairman of Campus Crusade for Christ*

Trust Him for peace to guard your heart…

_____

_____

_____

_____

_____

Accept His answer.

_____

_____

_____

_____

_____

Amen.

Notes

Notes

step eight

Producing Fruit

In East Tennessee where I grew up, each season has its own distinct beauty, but fall is the most inspiring. Each autumn the mountains are painted like fireworks as the leaves turn from summer's green to fluorescent shades of red, yellow, and orange. The splendor of the autumn season in this part of the country truly is spectacular to behold! From the deep reds of the oaks, to the brilliant oranges of the poplar trees, to the many shades and hues of the maples, God has displayed His splendor in a special way that time of year. I'm not what you would call an expert when it comes to trees, but I do know some of their names. I know an apple tree, because I can see the apples hanging on it. The same is true for peach, pear, and cherry trees. I know oaks by their acorns and walnut and hickory trees by the nuts they bear. I know dogwood trees by their blossoms in spring and berries in fall. I know maples by the helicopter seeds they bear each fall, and I can even spot some trees by the shapes of their leaves. But I would be at a loss to identify many at all though in the winter when the branches are bare, because I am not well studied enough to identify trees by their bark or shape. Like I said, I'm not an expert. I just love the woods, and I've picked up a thing or two over the years by the time I've spent there. You see, it is that which the tree bears that helps me to identify it.

"Each tree is known by its own fruit...."
—Luke 6:44

When Jesus told the parable we find in John 15 of the vine and the branches, the obvious main point He was making was that we are to stay in connection with Him. At the same time, however, if we focus only on that, we may miss the point that there is an expected result to this abiding. If we walk in fellowship with God, it will be manifested by the presence of what the Bible calls "fruit." God will produce in our lives visible markers that identify us as His children. It was said of some of Jesus' disciples, *"Now as they observed the confidence of Peter and John and understood that they were uneducated and untrained men, they were amazed, and began to recognize them as having been with Jesus"* (Acts 4:13). Can it be said of those around us that we are followers of Jesus? Do others see a difference in our lives? That is what God desires. He wants to bear His fruit through us. And not just a little bit—He wants to bear "much fruit" in us (John 15:8).

Think about that term, "fruit." Jesus means by that word that there would be visible evidence in us of His working in our lives. But I think He means more than just that. If you think very long about that word "fruit," your mind begins to conjure up images of delicious things. I think of tart, crunchy apples or juicy peaches. You see, it isn't just that our lives bear evidence of God, but that what they bear is attractive and beneficial to others. God created each of us to be a blessing to others. He wants to work in us, so that He can work through us in ways that minister. Ministry isn't just something reserved for the clergy. God wants every Christian to have a ministry. This week we want to look at evidence in John 15:7–8 that proves we are disciples of Jesus: that we bear much fruit.

Producing Fruit   DAY ONE

WHAT IS FRUIT?

We know what apples, oranges, peaches and bananas are. We easily recognize physical fruit. But what is "fruit" in a spiritual sense? If we are to bear fruit, we ought to have an understanding of what it is. Today, we want to look at a number of different passages in the Bible that use this word "fruit" and see what we can learn about what it is and is not.

📖 Looking at the verses that follow, identify what they teach about what biblical "fruit" is.

Galatians 5:22–23

_____

_____

_____

_____

Matthew 3:8

_____

_____

_____

_____

Ephesians 5:8–10

_____

_____

_____

_____

Do you see any common ground that these share?

_____

_____

_____

Think about what we learn here. The fruit mentioned in Galatians 5:22–23 are the character qualities produced in us as we abide with Christ—love, joy, peace, patience, kindness, goodness, faithfulness, gentleness, self-control. What an attractive person you and I become when Christ produces His character in us! In Matthew 3:8, Jesus speaks of bearing fruit _"in keeping with repentance."_ This indicates that a contrite and repentant heart about sin is one of the evidences of God working in us. Ephesians 5:8–10 tells us that we are to _"walk as children of light."_ The fruit of such a walk is expressed in _"all goodness and righteousness and truth."_ If God is at work in us, He will produce that which is good, right, and true. The commonality we see in each of these passages is a change in character.

📖 Looking at the verses that follow, identify what they teach about what biblical "fruit" is.

Romans 1:13

_____

_____

_____

Romans 15:28

_____

_____

_____

Colossians 1:10

_____

_____

_____

Do you see any common ground that these verses share?

_____

_____

_____

Not only does Jesus work changes in our character, but He also works through us to benefit others. In Romans 1:13 Paul seems to use the word

Did You Know?
FRUIT OF THE SPIRIT

Galatians 5:22–23 lists nine character qualities, but it speaks of them as the "fruit" of the Spirit, not the "fruits." Some commentators believe this singular reference means that the "fruit of the Spirit" is love, which is mentioned first. The other qualities expand on this and reveal the many different ways love manifests itself.

"fruit" to mean ministry results along the lines of evangelism and discipleship. Looking at Romans 15:28, one can see that fruit refers to the results of the believers' walk with God which, in this case, was an offering for impoverished believers in Jerusalem from the Christians in Macedonia and Achaia (the churches of Thessalonica, Phillipi, Berea, and Corinth as well as others). In Colossians 1:10 again fruit is linked with good works. The common thread in each of these passages is that as a result of God's work in our character, He desires to do a work in our communities as well—working through us in ministry what He has worked in us in maturity.

WHO IS SUPPOSED TO BEAR FRUIT?

Who is the minister at your church? Think before you answer that question, because how you answer it is very important. How your church answers this question is equally important. Sadly, the mindset of many churches is that the "clergy" are the ministers and the congregations are applauding spectators. Church life in a lot of places is much like a sporting event, where you have a handful of people in the action in desperate need of rest being cheered on by thousands in the stands in desperate need of exercise. But is that how God sees it? NO! The Scriptures make it very clear that God wants each of us to be a minister. Think about it. God wants each of us to live lives of spiritual fruitfulness. He wants to so work in us that He is able to work through us to the benefit of others.

📖 Read 1 Peter 4:10–11.

What does this passage say *"each one"* has received?

_____

_____

_____

What are they to do with what they have received?

_____

_____

_____

What different ways can we minister according to these verses?

_____

_____

_____

> ## "As each one has received a special gift, employ it in serving one another, as good stewards of the manifold grace of God."
>
> ### I Peter 4:10

This passage makes a powerful statement to all Christians. It tells us that **each one** of us has received a *"special gift."* These verses don't go into great detail about what that gift is, but we do know what we are to do with it— we are to employ it (put it to work) in serving others. In fact, it tells us that when we do, we are being good stewards of that gift. The next verse presents a couple of categories of gifts: speaking gifts and serving gifts. Whatever we do in service, God should be glorified in it.

The gifts Peter writes about are what we call "spiritual gifts." Every Christian has been given at least one, but none of us (except Jesus) has all of them. If you think about it, these truths make two guarantees:

1) Knowing that each of us has at least one gift assures us that **the Church needs us.** It won't be all it could be without what we have to offer.

2) Knowing that no one has all the gifts makes certain that **we need the Church.** We need what others have to give. God has designed the body of Christ (the Church) in such a way as to guarantee inter-dependence.

📖 Look at Romans 12:1–8. What must happen first before we can know God's will for our lives? (12:1–2)

_____

_____

_____

How do verses 3–5 explain that God has made the Church?

_____

_____

_____

What are we to do with our gifts? (verse 6a)

_____

_____

_____

What different ways can a Christian serve? (verses 6–8)

_____

_____

_____

Before we can know God's will for our lives, we must first put ourselves at His disposal. We must offer ourselves to be used by Him. Once we are willing to be used, He will show us His good, acceptable, and perfect will for where and how. In verses 3–5, we clearly see several important truths: **a)** God has given each of us a measure of faith, **b)** the Church is like the human body with many different parts, **c)** the parts of the body don't all have the same function. Verses 6–8 begin to show us some of those differences. This passage lists seven different spiritual gifts—grace endowments for service—that enable us to be useful in the Church and the Church's mission. Each of us has one of these gifts, but none have them all. Whichever God has given us in His grace, we are to exercise it in the body. You see, we did nothing to earn these spiritual gifts since they are given by God's grace. Neither can we change our giftedness by our own efforts. Our giftedness comes only by God's sovereign choice.

Most biblical scholars see the passage in Romans 12 as the main list of gifts—the motivational or service gifts. The Bible talks of other gifts than those listed here, but it seems through these abiding gifts that we minister, day-in

Word Study
GRACE GIFTS

The Greek word for "grace" (*charis*) is also the root of the word for spiritual gifts (*charisma*). The suffix *ma* in Greek means "the results of," and *charisma* means "the results of grace." We did nothing to earn our spiritual giftedness, nor can we change it by self-effort. It is a result of God's grace.

The Bible speaks of spiritual gifts in four different New Testament passages. Take some time to look up these Scriptures.

- **Romans 12**
- **1 Corinthians 12**
- **Ephesians 4**
- **1 Peter 4**

and day-out. These gifts include **prophecy** (speaking forth for God), **service** (serving others practically), **teaching** (instruction), **exhortation** (motivation and encouragement), **giving** (both financial and in other ways), **leading** (at many different levels), and **mercy** (compassion and care). These gifts are the main ways we serve each other in the body of Christ.

As you look at the list of spiritual gifts here in Romans 12, do you have any idea what your own spiritual gift is?

_____

_____

_____

If you don't know what your spiritual gift(s) is, don't worry. It will become evident over time. Your gift(s) isn't just what you do; it is a part of who you are. It will manifest itself in the kinds of service you enjoy, the types of serving you do that God blesses, the serving others affirm you in, and the opportunities God gives you. When you are serving in your giftedness, it will energize you, not drain you. And when you serve in your giftedness, others will benefit. The main things you need to understand are that God wants to use you and He has made you useable. Every Christian is supposed to bear fruit.

Producing Fruit | **DAY THREE**

YOU ARE ESSENTIAL

"For the body is not one member, but many. If the foot should say, 'Because I am not a hand, I am not a part of the body,' it is not for this reason any the less a part of the body. And if the ear should say, 'Because I am not an eye, I am not a part of the body,' it is not for this reason any the less a part of the body. If the whole body were an eye, where would the hearing be? If the whole were hearing, where would the sense of smell be? But now God has placed the members, each one of them, in the body, just as He desired. And if they were all one member, where would the body be? But now there are many members, but one body. And the eye cannot say to the hand, 'I have no need of you'; or again the head to the feet, 'I have no need of you.' On the contrary, it is much truer that the members of the body which seem to be weaker are necessary; and those members of the body, which we deem less honorable, on these we bestow more abundant honor, and our unseemly members come to have more abundant seemliness."
(1 Corinthians 12:14–23)

WE ARE EACH PART OF A BODY

Every Christian has a spiritual gift. Every believer is part of the church, the "body" of Christ. Sometimes we look at those with particular gifts and wish we were like them. But where would the body be if we all were the same? Where would the human body be with five noses and no ears? Where would it be with all hands and no feet? What good would it be to have three stomachs if you didn't have a heart? God has made the human body so that each part is needed and has made the Church the same way. A body can function without ears or feet, but not as effectively. However, some parts are so essential that there would be no life without them. And together, all these body parts make something they could never be separately. A heart is useless without blood vessels. A stomach is useless without a mouth. What a wonderful thing it is to know that we are all needed in the body of Christ! What value and significance this truth places on even the most unimportant looking parts!

📖 Look at Ephesians 4:11–12.

What spiritual gifts do you see here (verse 11)?

_____

_____

_____

What are these gifts to do (verse 12)?

_____

_____

What is the result of these gifts being exercised (verse 12)?

_____

_____

_____

_____

Paul tells us here that God has given certain gifted individuals to the Church. Their role is not to do all the works of service, but to "equip" the saints so that they can serve. In other words, these gifted people (each of the roles is identified elsewhere in Scripture as a leadership role) are to help each of us "saints" in the body be able to serve. We all have spiritual gifts. Verse 7 reminds us *"to each one of us grace was given."* But these gifts need to be developed, and that is the purpose of the leaders in the Church. As a result of their equipping ministry, we are able to serve, and the body of Christ (the Church) is built up. It becomes what God wants it to be.

📖 Take a look at Ephesians 4:15–16.

How is the body *"fitted and held together"*?

_____

_____

_____

What causes the body to grow?

_____

_____

_____

The Church is called the body of Christ. That body is both *"fitted and held together"* by that which every joint supplies. Maybe you don't consider yourself a joint, but the next part of Ephesians 4:15–16 makes it obvious that this idea applies to you. It says that it is the *"proper working of each individual part"* that causes the growth and building up of the body. In other words, the body of Christ won't be all it is supposed to be apart from you, for you are wanted and needed!

This idea of the Church as the "body" of Christ is more than mere imagery. Think about the underlying message. When Jesus walked on earth, He was seen and heard—He made a difference! But what about today? He is in heaven now, so is He no longer seen and heard? Of course He is still seen and heard in us this very day! What Jesus was as an individual back then, the Church is as an entity today. When each of us plays his or her part and serves as God has gifted us under the direction of Christ (the head [verse 15]), then Jesus is seen today! When the parts of the body move, coordinated by the direction of the head, needs can be met; ministry can happen; lives can be changed—the world can be affected!

We are each parts of an incredibly significant whole. Our contribution is needed, our input valued and desired. We can aid in making Jesus seen in a needy world. There is no room for feelings of insignificance on the part of any Christian. This is the point Jesus was making when He spoke of John

Extra Mile

CHRIST AS HEAD OF THE CHURCH

Christ is referred to as the "head" of the body (the church) in each of these passages:

- I Corinthians 11:3
- Ephesians 1:22
- Ephesians 4:15
- Ephesians 5:23
- Colossians 1:18
- Colossians 2:10
- Colossians 2:19

With this imagery, Christ is understood as the intelligence of the church, the source of direction, the guide of all the activities of the body, just as the brain is to the human body.

the Baptist. He claimed that of those *"born of women"* there is no one greater than John. But He went on to say, *"Yet he who is least in the kingdom of God is greater than he"* (Matthew 11:11; Luke 7:28). Jesus was showing the significance of those who are not only born of woman, but also born again of the Spirit of God. Though you may consider yourself the very least of these, Jesus says even the least is greater than John the Baptist!

Producing Fruit **DAY FOUR**

HOW DOES GOD WANT TO USE US?

Have you ever thought about why you are here on planet earth? If heaven is the very best place for the Christian, then why aren't we there already? Since God is all-powerful, it would be a simple thing for Him to take us there. Why don't we go straight to heaven when we become Christians? Why do we have to stay down here in a fallen world, waging war with sin and temptation? Why do we stay here struggling with sickness, aging, and death? If heaven is the place with no tears, no death, no pain, and no sin, why are we here? The answer to all these questions is that God has a purpose for the rest of our time on planet earth—and it isn't to make money. God leaves us here because He wants others to come to know His love and mercy through our witness. God's ultimate best is for us to be with Him in heaven, but right now, He has something planned for us that is equally important. He wants to work through us on earth so that others can join us in eternity.

📖 The apostle Paul seemed to be debating these very questions in his letter to the church at Philippi. Read Philippians 1:21–25 and write down what you learn.

_____

_____

_____

_____

Paul wrote this letter to Philippi from prison, and he seemed to be debating whether or not he would get out of there alive. In this consideration, he gives us a good list of the benefits both of living and of dying. To die, he says, is gain. In verse 23 he calls it *"very much better."* Yet he also recognized that to live would mean fruitful labor (verse 22). Getting specific as to what that labor would be in verse 25, he states that his living on and serving Christ would result in the joy and progress in the faith of others. To be in heaven would be better, but to remain on earth for a time is necessary. It is our remaining that allows us to minister to others.

📖 Look at 2 Corinthians 5:19–21.

Since Christ died for us, what should be our appropriate response (verse 15)?

_____

_____

_____

Word Study
"TO LIVE IS CHRIST"

In the Greek language there are two primary words for life: *bios* (from which we get our term "biology"—study of life in general) and *zōē* (from which we get our term "zoology"—study of higher life forms). It is this second word the apostle Paul uses here. *Zōē* generally points to quality of life as opposed to mere existence. This is the word Jesus used in John 10:10 when He said *"I came that they might have life"*—not just mere existence, but a higher quality of life. When Paul says *"to live is Christ"* (Philippians 1:21), he means to really live and not just to exist.

What did God do with us after He reconciled us to Himself through Christ (verses 18–19)?

_____

_____

_____

What ideas does it communicate that we are God's ambassadors (verse 20)?

_____

_____

_____

Christ died for us to free us from the burden of sin, not so that we could continue to wallow in it. He died for us to free us from selfish living. He liberated us so we could live for Him instead of for ourselves. Part of that living is woven into the ministry of reconciliation He has given to us. He wants to use us to help others be reconciled to Him. In fact, Christ has made us His ambassadors. Think about that. An ambassador is someone who lives in a foreign country so that he can represent his home country there. Not living for himself, but for the one he represents, he speaks the words and wishes of his native land to a foreign government. In the same way, earth is not our home. It is the assignment of our ambassadorship. It is the place we serve on behalf of the place that truly is our home: heaven.

One of the ways God wants to minister through us is by us representing Him to those who don't know Him. But there is more.

📖 Look at Matthew 28:18–20. What else does God want us to do?

_____

_____

_____

_____

God has given us the task of making disciples of all the nations. This task does not merely encompass evangelism. Conversion is not enough. God wants people to be made into disciples or followers of Him. He wants them to observe His commands and to identify with Him and His people. He wants each of us to help with that.

Biblical fruit involves us becoming more like Christ in our character, and as a result, we are to participate in His work—the work of evangelism and discipleship. Now, each one of us will not do this in exactly the same way. Our giftedness comes into play here.

Have you ever thought about the role spiritual giftedness plays in evangelism? We know that Ephesians 4 mentions *"evangelist"* as one of the positions of church leadership. Does this mean that some are gifted for evangelism and the rest of us keep quiet? Certainly not! Jesus makes it clear in Acts 1:8 that one of the results of the Spirit coming is that we would all be His witnesses. Giftedness does not determine if we will share Christ; all are called to that. What giftedness determines is how we will gain the opportunity to share Christ. Think of your spiritual gift as the key that opens the door for

"But you shall receive power when the Holy Spirit has come upon you; and you shall be My witnesses both in Jerusalem, and in all Judea and Samaria, and even to the remotest part of the earth."

Acts 1:8

you to share. If you are gifted with mercy, then most often it will be your showing of mercy that makes the unbeliever open to hear what you have to say about Christ. If you are gifted with service, then it will often be your serving that makes others want to listen to what you have to say. If you are gifted with giving, then giving will be a key that opens doors to the gospel. Whatever your giftedness is, most often that is the very thing that will provide you with opportunities to share Christ. I have led more people to Christ while simply teaching the Scriptures in a group setting than I have through one-on-one evangelism. It is through the exercise of our giftedness that God enables us to share Christ. What is your giftedness? That is where you need to look for opportunities to share the gospel! That is how God wants to bear fruit through you.

Producing Fruit **DAY FIVE**

FOR ME TO FOLLOW GOD

Jesus said, *"Follow Me, and I will make you fishers of men"* (Matthew 4:19). When we follow Him, He works changes in our lives. He changes our character, our values, and our priorities. As a result, He transforms us from selfish living that uses others for our own gain, into selfless living that seeks to be a blessing to others. In divine irony, God has so structured life that living for ourselves guarantees that our deepest needs go unmet, while living for others instead of self puts us in a place where the deep needs of our heart can be met. It is a lifestyle of faith. When we stop living only for self and trust God with our own needs, He not only meets them, but also uses us to meet them in others. God made each of us to be ministers. We are designed to be bearers of fruit, and we will be happy only when we are hearers.

Consider your own growth in Christ. Jesus wants you to be a disciple—to abide in Him and allow His words to abide in you. He wants you to ask, and He wants to answer your prayers. He wants your life to glorify God. And He wants all of that to culminate in your life bearing much fruit.

APPLY As you look at your Christian life so far, what are some evidences you see of Christ making changes in your character?

_____

_____

_____

_____

Look at the list of the *"fruit of the Spirit"* from Galatians 5:22–23. Think about each area, and ask yourself, "Has God changed me any in this area?"

Love

_____

_____

_____

_____

Joy

_____

_____

_____

_____

Peace

_____

_____

_____

_____

Patience

_____

_____

_____

_____

Kindness

_____

_____

_____

_____

Goodness

_____

_____

_____

_____

Faithfulness

_____

_____

_____

_____

Gentleness

_____

_____

_____

_____

"But the fruit of the Spirit is love, joy, peace, patience, kindness, goodness, faithfulness, gentleness, self-control; against such things there is no law."

Galatians 5:22–23

Self-Control

_____

_____

_____

_____

What are some evidences of His working through you for the benefit of others?

_____

_____

_____

_____

What do you think your main spiritual gift might be?

_____

_____

_____

How can you develop that gift?

_____

_____

_____

_____

What do you think your main spiritual gift is?

Do not be discouraged if you long for more fruit than is yet evident. Fruit is not just the immediate results of your pursuit of God. It is also a gradual result of maturing. The longer you walk with the Lord, the more fruit you will bear. The key is to focus on the foundation, not the fruit.

Consider the five areas of John 15:7–8 and rate how you think you are doing.

ABIDING IN HIM
Not doing well   1   2   3   4   5   Doing well

HIS WORDS ABIDING IN YOU
Not doing well   1   2   3   4   5   Doing well

ASKING AND GETTING ANSWERS
Not doing well   1   2   3   4   5   Doing well

GLORIFYING GOD
Not doing well   1   2   3   4   5   Doing well

BEARING MUCH FRUIT
Not doing well   1   2   3   4   5   Doing well

The key to fruitfulness is not found in focusing on working more or working harder, but in walking more closely. It is not the job of the branch to produce fruit, but rather to bear it as a result of staying connected to the vine.

The main things that keep us in fellowship with God are these: **1)** pursuing a relationship with Him through prayer and His Word, and **2)** dealing with sin as He reveals it by confessing and repenting.

As you close this week's lesson, write out a prayer to the Lord that reflects your heart on these two keys to abiding.

_____

_____

_____

_____

_____

_____

_____

_____

_____

_____

_____

_____

_____

_____

_____

_____

_____

_____

Notes

step nine

Faith

I can still remember from my childhood that place on the laundry room doorway where my mother marked off how tall I was. Alternately encouraged by focusing on my progress or discouraged by focusing on the advancement of my older brother, I can remember comparing my height with that of my brother's as well as with my own height at a younger age. We have a similar site on the wall in our laundry room. It is filled with the names of our kids and lines and dates. You see, it is good to be able to measure our progress in life. We need to measure our spiritual growth as well, not for the sake of comparing ourselves to others, but for the sake of seeing that we are making progress in the areas that count. With this lesson we want to begin looking at some biblical yardsticks for measuring our progress in the Christian life. I don't want this to discourage you, for you may not be as far along as someone who has been a Christian for a long time or one who has been pursuing his or her relationship with Christ diligently the whole time he or she has been a Christian. I just want to help you see the main areas on which you should focus.

In 1 Corinthians 13:13 the apostle Paul writes, *"But now abide faith, hope, love, these three; but the greatest of these is love."* If I can paraphrase this verse for you, I'd put it this way: "Three things

"But now abide faith, hope, love, these three; but the greatest of these is love."

1 Corinthians 13:13

really matter in life—faith, hope, and love—and love is the most important of the three." If these are the things that really matter, then these are the things that ought to really matter **to us.** We ought to be concerned about how we are doing in each of these three areas. We ought to check ourselves from time to time to see if we are making progress. And we ought to be honest enough to admit where we need to grow. Hopefully this lesson (and the two that follow) will be a help to you in that regard.

Faith DAY ONE

A BIBLICAL YARDSTICK TO MEASURE BY

When Paul listed faith, hope, and love as the three things that last, he did so in the context of correcting a church that was not what it should have been. The Corinthian church was out of balance. They had all the gifts, but they weren't using them properly. Their church services must have been chaos. Everyone was focused on self instead of Christ. They were bumping over each other to exercise their gifts—not for the sake of ministry—but for the sake of self-glory. Paul warned them that if they spoke like the greatest of men or even like angels but didn't have love, they were just making noise. In fact, he devoted a whole chapter just to talking about love, because it was so lacking in that church. At the end of that chapter, he highlighted love as the most important thing, but he also highlighted two other important areas: faith and hope. These weren't just religious terms to Paul. They were the measure of spiritual health.

📖 Look at 1 Thessalonians 1:2–3.

For what is Paul thankful?

The Thessalonians work produced by faith, labor prompted by love & endurance inspired by hope.

Why do you think Paul is thankful for these things specifically?

These are evidences of their spirituality, of their growth.

It is interesting that Paul would commend the church at Thessalonica for the three things he told the Corinthians were of utmost importance (and were obviously lacking at Corinth). Clearly Paul saw them as signs of spiritual health (or the lack of it).

📖 Read Colossians 1:3–5. For what does Paul commend the church at Colosse?

The Colossians faith in Christ, love for the saints, & hope stored up for them in heaven.

Extra Mile

FAITH, HOPE, AND LOVE

The apostle Paul wrote about half of the New Testament. The books he wrote are called epistles (the cultural term for letters) because they were letters he wrote to individuals and churches. In almost every letter he wrote, he emphasized three attributes: faith, hope, and love. Take some time to read the following passages where these three attributes are mentioned.

- **I Corinthians 13:13**
- **Colossians 1:4–5**
- **I Thessalonians 1:3**
- **I Thessalonians 5:8**
- **2 Thessalonians 1:3–5**
- **I Timothy 1:1–5**
- **I Timothy 1:14–16**
- **2 Timothy 1:12–13**
- **Titus 2:2, 13**

Again we see these same three things commended: faith, hope, and love. Clearly Paul saw these as the keys to a healthy church.

To really appreciate each of the members of this trio, we need to know what the three words mean. Faith (*pistis*) has the idea of trusting God and what He says. At its core, it means to take God at His word and act accordingly. Trust is a good synonym. Hope (*elpis*) isn't merely hoping something will happen, but in a spiritual sense, it speaks of our future hope—looking with an eternal perspective. Paul encourages us to be looking for the "blessed hope" of Christ's return for His people (Titus 2:13). Practically speaking, it means to live for eternity, instead of just living for the passing pleasures of this world. Love (*agapē*) doesn't just embody charitable feelings or care. *Agape* speaks of the unconditional love that God has and that He enables in His followers. These three attributes are the most important in measuring how mature we are.

Think about how the triad of faith, hope, and love measure our spiritual maturity. Are we trusting God in the situations of our day-to-day life? Are we living like heaven is our home and our hope? Are we loving others as God desires us to? These are the spiritual values that really matter.

WHAT IS FAITH?

There is a lot of talk today about faith, especially in religious circles, but there still exists a great deal of confusion about what it is. In defining what true faith is, we need to begin by defining what it is not. Faith is grounded in fact, not mere *impressions*. It is not our believing (hoping or wishing) that something will or will not happen that determines the outcome. It is what God wills. The great saint and missionary George Mueller said, "Impressions have neither one thing nor the other to do with faith. Faith has to do with the Word of God. It is not impressions, strong or weak, which will make the difference. We will have to do with the written Word and not ourselves or our impressions." Having faith is not the same thing as depending upon a probability. To believe because something is likely is no more faith than to disbelieve because something is unlikely. Mueller also said, "Many people are willing to believe regarding those things that seem probable to them. Faith has nothing to do with probabilities. The province of faith begins where probabilities cease and sight and sense fail. Appearances are not to be taken into account. The question is whether God has spoken it in His Word."

Biblical faith is not about what we think or hope will happen, nor is it about what seems likely to happen. It is about what God has said will happen. It is about the certainties of what God has spoken. Someone once defined faith as this: "God said it. I believe it. That settles it!" It is choosing to believe what God says that settles issues in our lives. Before we can exercise faith, it must have an object. The object of our faith is to be God Himself as He is revealed in the Bible. Without knowing what God says, there can be no true faith. Faith is so much more than positive thinking—striving to believe hard enough, thinking that if we do so, we can make it come to pass. True faith must have facts to rest on. So how do we find such faith?

> "Many people are willing to believe regarding those things that seem probable to them. Faith has nothing to do with probabilities . . . The question is—whether God has spoken it in His Word."
>
> —George Mueller

📖 Look at 2 Corinthians 13:5.

What does this verse instruct us to do?

Examine ourselves - realize Jesus is in us.

How do we know for sure if we are in the faith?

If we have placed our trust in Christ, then we are in the faith.

Paul instructs us to examine ourselves to see if we are *"in the faith."* In other words, we need to be sure we have a relationship with God. This is not merely about believing that Jesus existed or that He died for us. True biblical faith means we have placed our trust in Him for our salvation. We know we are "in the faith" if Christ indeed lives in us. First John 5:11–13 tells us, *"And the witness is this, that God has given us eternal life, and this life is in His Son. He who has the Son has the life; he who does not have the Son of God does not have the life. These things I have written to you who believe in the name of the Son of God, in order that you may know that you have eternal life."* It is possible to know that we have eternal life—if Jesus is in our lives. We cannot exercise biblical faith if we have never received Christ. The beginning of faith is entering into Christ's realm.

Where Does Faith Originate?

📖 Read Romans 10:17. What does this verse teach about the origin of faith in our lives?

Originates through hearing the word of God.

Biblical faith comes from the Bible. Genuine faith is originated when we hear the Word of God. Christ living in our hearts affirms the message, and we are able to choose to trust what God says. Real faith is based solely on biblical facts. If our faith is based on anything other than the Word of God, then it is either presumption, speculation, or superstition. The obvious application is that if faith comes from hearing the Word of God, then we ought to be spending regular time in the Word.

📖 Consider Hebrews 12:2. According to this verse, where does faith originate?

Jesus

> **"Fixing our eyes on Jesus, the author and perfecter of faith, who for the joy set before Him endured the cross, despising the shame, and has sat down at the right hand of the throne of God."**
>
> **Hebrews 12:2**

This verse teaches us that Jesus is both the author (beginner) and the perfecter (completer) of faith. Biblical faith does not originate with us. It comes from Christ. If you want more faith, look to Him, not to yourself. Faith begins with Him, and it is perfected with Him. Our faith grows as our relationship with Christ grows.

The Faith Principle

What is faith? It is making choices to act on what we believe. We exercise faith regularly in the physical realm. Every time we sit in a chair, we put our faith in it. We trust that it will hold us up, and therefore we are willing to put weight on it. When we climb into an airplane, we are actively trusting that it will get us where we need to go. The same is true in the spiritual realm. Faith is not merely idle intellectual fancy. It is the choice to place our trust in God, to take God at His word and act accordingly.

A century ago, the most famous tightrope walker was a man named Charles Blondin. Everywhere he went, he astounded audiences with his balance and agility on a high wire. On one occasion, Blondin performed the amazing feat of walking across a rope spanning the basin of Niagara Falls. Not only did he walk across without the security of a net, but he also pushed a wheelbarrow across. The crowd cheered with awed amazement! Then he asked if they believed he could push a person across in the wheelbarrow. They enthusiastically shouted, "Yes!" Nevertheless, the crowd got strangely quiet when he asked for volunteers. You see, it was one thing for the crowd to acknowledge that Blondin could push a person across. That took no real faith, for they had already witnessed him perform spectacular feats and had confidence that he was capable of doing more. However, it was quite another matter to trust him enough to put their lives in his hands. Finally, a small girl stepped forward and volunteered. It was Blondin's daughter. She knew her daddy was trustworthy, and so she exercised faith in him. This illustration is at the core of what true, biblical faith is. It is not merely an intellectual belief that God **can** do something, but a decision to trust that He **will** do it. The main issue of faith is not how much of it we have, but where we place it. Is the object of our trust trustworthy? Charles Blondin was a very gifted and experienced tightrope walker, but he eventually met his death in a fall. A chair with unsteady legs will not hold us up regardless of how hard we believe in it. God, however, is worthy of our trust, and He takes great delight in the trust of His children.

📖 Read through 2 Corinthians 5:7 and answer the questions that follow.

What do you think it means to "walk by faith"?

_____

_____

_____

_____

_____

HOW MUCH FAITH IS ENOUGH?

Jesus said, *"Truly I say to you, if you have faith as a mustard seed, you shall say to this mountain, 'Move from here to there,' and it shall move; and nothing shall be impossible to you"* (Matthew 17:20). The mustard seed was the smallest seed commonly known in the area of Israel. Jesus' point was that it isn't how much faith you have that is important but whether that faith is placed in Him.

What do you think it would be to "walk by sight"?

_____

_____

_____

_____

The term "walk" paints an interesting picture. It emphasizes not a single step or leap, but a lot of steps put together. Faith is not just for salvation; it is for living day by day. God wants us to trust Him with everything that happens in our lives. He wants us to take Him at His word—that what He says is true, really is true; that what He says He will do, He really will do. He doesn't want us to walk by sight, for that would mean we would never act on what God says in the Bible unless we could figure everything out.

📖 Look at Galatians 3:11 and write what you learn there about living by faith.

_____

_____

_____

_____

Faith is a fundamental of the Christian life. Galatians 3:11 makes it clear that living by faith is a righteous thing. God wants us to live by faith. This verse is a quote from the Old Testament book of Habakkuk where living by faith is contrasted with the proud one who trusts in himself. It is also quoted in Romans 1:17 and Hebrews 10:38 which adds, _"And if he shrinks back, My soul has no pleasure in him."_ God wants us to live by faith.

📖 Read Hebrews 11:6 and write what you learn there about faith.

_____

_____

_____

_____

"And without faith it is impossible to please Him, for he who comes to God must believe that He is, and that He is a rewarder of those who seek Him."

Hebrews 11:6

Hebrews 11:6 makes it clear that it is impossible to be pleasing to God without faith. This verse points out two paramount principles of what faith is. First, we must believe that God is—that He exists, and that He is who the Scriptures say He is. Second, we must trust that He rewards those who seek Him. When we understand this, we will want to involve Him in every area of our lives. We can't please Him if we are unwilling to trust Him in the details of life.

📖 Take a look at Romans 14:23 and write what you learn there about this issue of faith.

_____

_____

_____

_____

Romans 14:23 shows us the flip side of faith—whatever is not flowing out of faith is sin. We usually think of sin as things we do that God says not to do, but sin is also our refusal to trust God and His Word. Sometimes this sin manifests itself in that we don't do what we should.

God wants His children to live lives of trust in Him. He wants us to be willing to take Him at His word, and actively trust the things He says. How we succeed at trusting God and His promises in our daily life, is one of the measures of how we are doing spiritually.

PRACTICING FAITH

Faith is like a muscle; it grows with use, and it atrophies if it isn't used. The diagram in the sidebar illustrates how faith grows. The solid circle represents my present faith. Anything that falls inside the circle is something I'm able to trust God to do and have actually seen Him do. Those things outside the circle are what God can do, but I've never trusted Him to do. If I don't exercise my present faith, my circle of confidence (what I can trust God with) shrinks, and I find it harder and harder to trust Him. As long as I exercise my present faith, it remains the same. It doesn't grow, but it doesn't diminish either. In order for my faith to grow, I must step outside this circle of present confidence and trust God to do things the Word says He can but for which I have never trusted Him. As I do this, the circle of my faith (confidence in God) grows, and it's easier to trust Him to do as much next time.

📖 Look up the verses listed below and write what you understand about the three different kinds of faith.

Ephesians 2:8–9

_____

_____

_____

Jude 1:3

_____

_____

_____

2 Corinthians 5:7

_____

_____

_____

**THE EVER-EXPANDING
CIRCLE OF FAITH**

When the Bible speaks of faith, it refers to it in three different but related ways. In Ephesians 2:8–9 we are told that we are saved by grace through faith. "Saving faith" is the initial choice to trust the gospel message and receive God's gift of salvation through Christ. Jude 1:3 speaks of contending earnestly for *"the faith."* Here, faith has the idea of the whole of Christian doctrine—that which we believe as Christians. We must make a choice to believe what God says is truth—this is "doctrinal faith." Second Corinthians 5:7 says we *"walk by faith."* This speaks of the choices we make to trust God situation by situation as we walk through life. This "walking faith" always stands on the foundation of "saving" and "doctrinal" faith. We cannot trust God day by day with the circumstances of life if we have never trusted Him for salvation or if we do not believe what He says is truth—the doctrines of the Bible. That is why living faith is a growing thing. We trust God more as we learn more about Him.

📖 Read Hebrews 11:1 and record what you learn there about faith.

_____

_____

_____

_____

_____

_____

The Bible defines faith as being sure of what we hope for and certain of what we do not see (Hebrews 11:1). What this means for Christians is that even through we may not fully understand what is going on around us, we can have confidence that God is completely trustworthy and has our best interests in mind at all times. For example, an airline pilot may have his view obscured by clouds, but he has been trained to rely on his instrument panel to give him the accurate information and direction he needs to safely navigate his course.

In a similar way, the follower of Christ is to live by faith in God and His Word on a daily basis. The late Manley Beasley used to define faith in this way:

> *Faith is living as though the Bible is true,*
> *even when I do not feel it is true.*
> *The reason I can live as though it*
> *is true is because it is true.*
> *The reason it is true is because God says it is true.*

Faith is depending on God, and this begins only where depending on self ends. Sadly, for many of us, depending on ourselves is such an ingrained habit that it only is put aside when we come to the end of ourselves. Therefore, God must break us before we will trust Him. He must engineer our circumstances to bring us to the end of ourselves, or else we will never experience the blessings of faith. What He desires though, is that we mature to the point of trusting Him by choice and not merely by necessity.

Most likely, today, and every day you encounter situations where you could and should trust God. It may be in relationships, business, finances, or some other facet of life. Trusting God is always a choice. It is finding what God says about your situation in the Scriptures, and then choosing to act on that in faith.

📖 Proverbs 30:5 says, *"Every word of God is tested; He is a shield to those who take refuge in Him."* Reflect on this truth for a minute and then write your thoughts below.

_____

_____

_____

_____

Any law of science is not relied upon until it has been thoroughly tested and shown to be true. What a comfort it is to know that literally **every word of God** has been tested in the crucible of human experience and proven to be true. The Hebrew word for "tested" has the idea of refined precious metal without any impurities (hence the King James Version translates it "pure").

The result to us is significant. Because every word of God is proven true, His promises provide a shield of protection and a place of refuge for us. Oh, the promises themselves aren't mystical; but as they show us truth about God, they show us how (and when) to take refuge in Him. Peter tells us, *"He has granted to us His precious and magnificent promises, in order that by them you might become partakers of the divine nature"* (2 Peter 1:4).

The only problem with the shield of God's truth arises when we don't hide behind it. Our verse tells us *"He is a shield to those who take refuge in Him."* A shield is useless till you hide behind it. During the Vietnam war "flack jackets" (a type of bulletproof vest) were standard issue to most infantrymen. Because of the hot, humid, jungle conditions, the jackets were often unworn, and tragically many soldiers lost their lives because they weren't making use of the protection available to them. In the same way, the provision and protection of God's promises are of no benefit to us unless we take refuge in them, and we can't take refuge in them until we learn them and begin applying them. *"He is a shield to those who take refuge in Him."*

Did You Know?
GOD'S WORD AS A SHIELD

In the Roman Empire, soldiers made use of large shields tall enough to hide behind. When under duress, they would line their shields up so that they would touch each other. Then they would stoop behind them so they could advance while being protected from the arrows of the enemy. The Bible pictures the words of God as such a shield. But as with any shield, it only benefits those who take refuge behind it.

FOR ME TO FOLLOW GOD

Faith  **DAY FIVE**

Abraham believed God, and it was credited to him as righteousness (Genesis 15:6). Abraham was not a perfect man or some saint who never sinned or stumbled. But he was willing to trust the things that God said, and that faith is what pleased God. Noah built the ark by faith (Hebrews 11:7). By faith, the Israelites kept the Passover, and their first-born children were spared when the death angel visited Egypt (Hebrews 11:28). It was faith in what God said that gave Joshua and Israel courage to march around Jericho, trusting that God was going to tear down the walls of that city (Hebrews 11:30). Faith in God motivated the prostitute Rahab to protect the spies of Israel (Hebrews 11:31). Faith too, was what enabled David to enter into battle with the giant, Goliath, and defeat him (Hebrews 11:32). "But I'm no David!" you may be saying. Listen to what Charles Swindoll says about these people:

> The men and women in faith's Hall of Fame weren't perfect. Most had weakness with which God had to deal. For example, Noah became

THE HALL OF FAITH

Hebrews 11 has often been called "Faith's Hall of Fame" for its listing of some of the most prominent characters of the Bible known for their faithfulness. But none of the people listed in this chapter were exactly perfect. In fact, they all had their own weaknesses and shortcomings. For instance:

- Noah became drunk and allowed shame and reproach to come to his family (Genesis 9:20–27).

- Abraham occasionally had trouble telling the truth, which brought harm to his wife Sarah and to others (Genesis 12:10–20; 20:1–18).

- Sarah laughed when told by God that she would give birth to a son at age 90 (Genesis 18:9–15).

- Jacob was a deceiver (Genesis 25:27–34; 27:1–46)

- Moses was guilty of murder (Exodus 2:11–15).

- Rahab was guilty of sexual misconduct (Joshua 2:1).

- Samson continually exhibited poor judgment and rash behavior (Judges 14:16).

These people in "Faith's Hall of Fame" were in many ways no different from you and me. They had their numerous faults, yet they believed that God would make good on His promises and learned to trust God instead of themselves.

drunk after the flood and was a shame to his family (Genesis 9:20–27). Abraham was given to lying on occasion, and often at his wife's expense he tried to save his own life (Genesis 12:10–20; 20:1–18). Sarah laughed when God told her she was going to give birth at age 90 (Genesis 18:9–15). Jacob was a chiseler and deceiver (Genesis 25:27–34; 27:1–46). Moses was a murderer who tried to hide the body of his Egyptian victim (Exodus 2:11–15). Rahab had a background of lust and promiscuity (Joshua 2:1). Samson lived with uncontrollable desires (Judges 14:16). These people simply believed that God existed in the situation they faced, and finally trusted Him and not themselves. (*Faith that Endures: In Times Like These*, Word Publishing, 1982, page 2).

God wants you to trust Him, just like those people did. He doesn't expect you to be perfect. You don't have to have a testimony of unshakable faith. You just need to be willing to place your shaky faith in the promises of an unshakable God.

APPLY What are some situations or barriers you are facing that require faith?

_____

_____

_____

_____

_____

What fears and emotions are you experiencing?

_____

_____

_____

_____

APPLY One of the things that help us trust God with the present is remembering how God has been faithful in the past, both in our lives and throughout history. What are some examples that you can think of?

_____

_____

_____

_____

_____

_____

Another thing that helps us trust God is knowing His attributes. There are many, but the three main ones are...

☑ **Omnipotence: He is all-powerful.**

☑ **Omnipresence: He is everywhere at once.**

☑ **Omniscience: He knows everything there is to know.**

Which of these attributes of God are needed in your present situation?

_____

_____

_____

_____

What actions do you need to take to trust God with your present challenges?

_____

_____

_____

_____

_____

Faith is not just an idea or an emotion. It is a choice. The more you use the faith you have, the more faith you will have. As you close this week's lesson, why not write out a prayer to Him expressing your desire to trust Him and if need be, confessing any struggles you are having in doing that.

_____

_____

_____

_____

_____

_____

_____

_____

_____

_____

_____

_____

_____

_____

_____

_____

_____

_____

_____

_____

_____

_____

Notes

Difficulties are food for faith to feed on.

Faith precedes understanding

Hope

What do you hope for? This word, "hope" is an interesting word. It has been so widely used in modern English as to erode its original meaning. Consider some common ways the word is used today. A farmer says, "I hope it rains." A teenage girl longingly wishes, "I hope he asks me out." An employee reflects, "I hope I get a raise this year." A young couple awaiting their child comments, "I hope it's a boy!" Hope has come to have the idea of desiring something that might possibly happen. When the Bible uses the term, it has a very different concept in mind. Biblical hope is the promised certainty of what God has said He will do. By this definition, it exists not in the realm of possibility or even probability, but in the realm of those things that are certain to happen, and are only future in the sense that they haven't happened yet. To God, who is not bound by time, future promise is just as certain as past history. We saw in the previous lesson that the measures of our maturity are faith, hope and love. This week we want to focus on that second measurement of hope.

The kind of hope the Bible refers to is very closely related to faith. In fact, the Old English meaning had more the idea of trust than it did wish. The difference between faith and hope

"Biblical hope is the promised certainty of what God has said He will do. By this definition, it exists not in the realm of possibility or even probability, but in the realm of those things that are certain to happen and are only future in the sense that they haven't happened yet."

really revolve around timing. Faith focuses more on trusting the Bible about the past, and trusting God with the present. Hope is trust that centers on the future—how willing we are we to trust what God has promised will happen. Hope points to Christ's return, to heaven, and to eternity. Our hope is as certain as the One in whom we hope. If our future hope truly is the Lord, then that hope makes changes in the way we live today. We live with an eye on eternity instead of living as if today is all there is. This kind of hope we speak about is closely related to what we believe, and how we behave in light of that belief. For this reason, it becomes a good measure of our spiritual maturity.

Hope **DAY ONE**

UNDERSTANDING OUR CHRISTIAN HOPE

Just as food, air, and water are essential for man's survival, so too is hope. Without hope, we cannot function well. It is hanging on to our hope in God that gives us the moral courage to obey His will and resist temptation. When we go through hard times, it is the hope of a better future that keeps us from despair. When we are tempted to step outside God's will, it is the hope of future reward (as well as judgment) that motivate us to make right choices instead of wrong ones. Unless we are *"looking for the blessed hope"* (Titus 2:13) of future glory, we are easy prey to discouragement and aimlessness. The Bible uses this same concept to describe the unbeliever. In Ephesians 2:12, Paul speaks of the Gentiles as *"having no hope and without God in the world."* I can remember what that was like. You know from earlier chapters that before I became a Christian, I was very involved in the drug culture and all that goes along with it. While most would not approve of such a lifestyle, abusing drugs makes sense if you have the worldview that I had. If you believe that there is no God and no eternity—that this life is all there is—then it doesn't make sense to deprive yourself of any pleasure this world offers; for this world and our brief time on it are the only hope we have. This concept is what Paul alludes to in 1 Corinthians 15:32 when he writes, *"If the dead are not raised, let us eat and drink, for tomorrow we die."* Much of the world today operates from this philosophy. But a growing Christian doesn't have to, for he has a better hope than this world.

📖 Read Titus 1:2 and answer the questions that follow.

What is our Christian hope?

Eternal life w/ Christ Build your life on the foundation of a trustworthy God who never lies.

What is the assurance of that hope?

Our hope as Christians is eternal life. Having eternal life does not merely mean that we will exist forever. Every human soul will exist forever. Some will experience eternal life in heaven, while others will experience eternal separation from God in hell. The Greek word for "life" used here (*zoe*) suggests not just an eternal existence but also an endearing quality of life. In other words, not only are we going to exist forever, but also we are really going to **live** during that time. The guarantee of this eternal life, which is our hope, is the fact that God Himself has promised it. Since He cannot lie, then everything He says comes to pass.

📖 Look at Titus 2:13. What event should we be anticipating?

Christ's return

As Christians, we should not live as if today is all there is. On the contrary, our focus ought to be on the future. We are called to be *"looking for the blessed hope"* which is Christ's return. The Bible promises that just as Jesus ascended to heaven after the resurrection, one day He will return in the same way to take us to heaven (Acts 1:9–11). Expecting that it could come soon, we are to live, looking forward to that day.

📖 Study 2 Corinthians 5:10. What will happen when Christ returns to earth?

We will be judged for what we have done or not done.

When Jesus returns, it will mean different things to different people. To unbelievers, Christ's coming will mean judgment for their rejection of Him. For believers however, Jesus will come back to reward them for their faithful service to Him. One of the reasons hope is so important is that focusing on it affects how you and I live. Knowing that a day of reward is coming motivates us to *"have as our ambition . . . to be pleasing to Him"* (2 Corinthians 5:9).

The Christian's hope is such a practical thing. It is based on what we believe about what God says concerning our future. We who trust what God says will live in light of eternity, and we cannot trust what God says about our future if we are unaware of it.

Doctrine

THE JUDGMENT SEAT OF CHRIST

The Greek word *bema* (judgment seat) refers to the Roman legal system and has in view the cultural picture of the bema platform in each town where judicial decisions were made. It was an intimidating sight because the judge would sit much higher than everyone else and the one on trial would have to look up at him. Here *bema* is related to the judgment of believers' works (1 Corinthians 3:10–15). In this judgment, it is not the person who is judged but his or her deeds, and not for salvation, but for reward.

DO YOU KNOW YOUR HOPE?

Hope **DAY TWO**

I magine that you are on vacation in Hawaii and one day you go on a three-hour tour by boat. The weather starts getting rough—the tiny ship is tossed. If not for the courage of the fearless crew, your boat would be lost. The ship finally sits aground on the shore of an uncharted desert isle, and you are stranded on Gilligan's Island with the skipper, Mary Ann, the professor, and company. Your one great goal is to be rescued. Yet as time goes by, and idea after idea fails, your expectation of being rescued begins to fade. You wonder if you ever will be taken out of your situation, and it begins to seem hopeless. For Gilligan and the others, the question about rescue is not

"I pray that the eyes of your heart may be enlightened, so that you may know what is the hope of His calling...."

Ephesians 1:18

about "when" but about "if." So you try to make the best of the situation. You weave a hammock from palm fronds. You make cups out of coconuts. Doing the best you can and wishing for something better, you don't really expect anything to change. Sadly, many Christians think of their future hope in the same terms. They don't know that their rescue from this present world is certain. They long to be rescued from this fallen place, stained as it is by the results of sin—war, sickness, fear, and death. But they don't live as if that rescue is assured or even likely. If we do not understand our Christian hope, then we may end up living like those who have no hope.

The apostle Paul had a parent's love and concern for the churches he started in different places. He wanted them to trust God and to love each other. And he wanted them to understand the hope of their future with God. Today we want to look at how he helped others understand their hope.

📖 Take a look at Ephesians 1:15–18.

What does Paul say he has heard that the Ephesians have (verse 15)?

Faith in the Lord
Love for the saints

What does he pray for them to have (verses 17–18)?

Spirit of wisdom + revelation so that they can know Him better

When Paul wrote his letter to the church at Ephesus, he commends those believers for their faith and love, but he prays for them in this area of hope. He prays that God would give light to the eyes of their hearts so they would know God better and understand the incredible hope they have for the future because of their relationship with Him. Paul was concerned that these Christians grow up in their understanding of the future plans of God for them.

You remember we spent the first lesson looking at Ephesians 1. The phrase *"hope of His calling"* accurately reflects what the first three chapters of Ephesians are all about. In chapter 2, Paul reminds the Ephesians of their hopeless state before they met Christ, but he also points their attention to the hope that was now theirs. The very fact that he prays for them in this area of hope is significant for several reasons.

📖 Look again at Ephesians 1:15–18.

What do you think it means for the *"eyes of your heart [to] be enlightened"*?

Inner awareness -- flooded with light to understand the hope. Eyes of your heart. Holy Spirit opening our heart to wisdom + understanding.

What does it say about the Ephesians that Paul prayed this?

First, Paul prays that the eyes of their hearts would be enlightened. Think about that. He isn't just concerned about their minds, but also their hearts. Sometimes we can be taught something, but it is just "head knowledge"— we know the information, but it really doesn't affect us. It hasn't yet reached our heart. Paul wants them not only to know intellectually of their hope, but also for it to be real in their hearts. The very fact that he prays this tells us that this was a need for the Ephesians. It is probably a need for you and me as well. We all need to appreciate more fully the hope that is ours in Christ.

As we consider maturing in our hope, we must recognize that maturity is not a static thing. We do not reach a point and simply stay there. We are always either progressing or regressing.

📖 Read 1 Thessalonians 1:3. For what does Paul commend them?

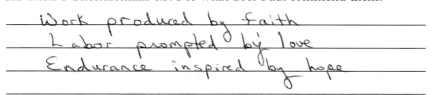

Work produced by faith
Labor prompted by love
Endurance inspired by hope

The Thessalonian church was obviously a healthy church. Paul holds them up as an example to others. He commends them for their work which resulted from faith, for their labor prompted by love, and for the endurance they had because of their hope. This was one of Paul's earliest letters to a church, and was probably written about A.D. 51. About a year or so later, Paul wrote them a second letter.

📖 Consider 2 Thessalonians 1:3–4.

For what does Paul commend them?

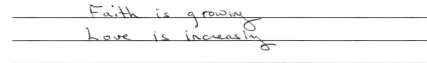

Faith is growing
Love is increasing

What is left out from the first list?

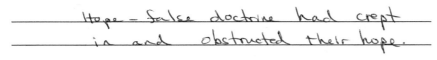

Hope – False doctrine had crept
in and obstructed their hope.

In his second letter, Paul commends them for their faith and love. In fact, he says that both of these attributes were increasing—they were making progress in those areas. Yet conspicuously absent from this list is any mention of how they were doing in the area of hope. Actually, if you read the whole letter you find the reason why: someone had confused the people with false doctrine about the Lord's return. They had ceased to have a clear view of their hope.

There is an important message for us in the experience of the Thessalonians. Just because we are doing well in an area today is no guarantee that we will be healthy in that area tomorrow. We must keep our hope in focus, or we will cease to live in light of it.

Put Yourself In Their Shoes

HOPE FOR EPHESIANS AND ALL CHRISTIANS

Those who don't know Christ are dead in their _"trespasses and sins"_ (Ephesians 2:1).

- following sinful lusts (2:3)
- headed for wrath (2:3)
- separate from Christ (2:12)
- excluded from God's people (2:12)
- strangers to the covenants of God's promises (2:12)
- without hope (2:12)

Those who know Christ are . . .

- made alive with Him (2:5)
- raised up with Christ and seated with Him in heaven (2:6)
- objects of grace (2:7)
- made one with Christ (2:14)
- fellow citizens (2:19)
- a dwelling place for God (2:22)

We must keep our hope in focus, or we will cease to live in light of it.

FALSE HOPES

Proverbs 13:12 tells us *"hope deferred makes the heart sick."* In other words, it is a horrible thing when you put your hope in something or someone and that person or thing lets you down. Unfortunately, people put their trust every day in things that will let them down. Just because you are a Christian, that does not make you immune to mistaken choices. The Bible talks a lot about our hope, but it also talks about false hopes—wrong places to put our trust. Let's look at some of them.

📖 What is the message of Psalm 33:17, and how do you think it applies to us today?

_____

_____

_____

_____

_____

Here, a horse is called a *"false hope for victory."* Keep in mind that the context of this verse is talking about being in a battle. In those days most of the soldiers fought on foot. To have a horse would seem to give an advantage, but God says that to trust in such things is a false hope. No matter how great our technology and weapons, no matter how big our army or how strong our men, these things alone cannot save us. If God is against us, nothing can help us; and if He is for us, no other helps will be needed. Verses 18–19 say, *"The eye of the LORD is on those who fear Him, on those who hope for His loving-kindness, to deliver their soul from death, and to keep them alive in famine."* Verse 20 says, *"He is our help and our shield."* We can use the best weapons we can find, but our hope should not be in them, but in God.

📖 What does Psalm 62:10 identify as a false hope?

_____

_____

_____

This psalm shows us that one who hopes in robbery to cause them to prosper hopes in vain. In other words, whatever we gain by striving outside the boundaries of the law will not really prosper us. We will eventually get caught—if not in this life, then in the next. But whatever temporary prosperity we find in such a way will not really be a blessing.

📖 Look at 1 Timothy 6:17 and identify what it teaches of true and false hopes.

_____

_____

_____

_____

Many there are who put their trust in riches, but God instructs us not to place our hope on something so uncertain. Rather, even when we are rich we are not to hope in that but in God. Luke 16:9 says, *"Make friends for yourselves by means of the mammon of unrighteousness; that when it fails, they may receive you into the eternal dwellings."* Notice it says not "if" it fails, but "when" it fails. Sooner or later money will let us down, but God won't.

📖 Read John 5:45 in its context.

In whom or what did the Pharisees place their hope?

_____

_____

What was the result of that hope?

_____

_____

_____

_____

The Pharisees put their trust for their salvation in the law of Moses. Yet Jesus makes it clear that the very law in which they were placing their hope would instead be the very source of their condemnation. They hoped in the law, and it was that same law that would convict them.

There are many places we put our hope, but Jesus is the only one that is secure.

THE EFFECTS OF HOPE

On January 3, 1956, Jim Elliot, Pete Fleming, Ed McCully, Nate Saint, and Roger Youderian boarded a Piper Cruiser plane, pursuing a dream of taking the gospel to tribal people in Ecuador who'd never heard. Their target people group was the savage Auca Indians, a tribe that had resisted all contact with outsiders. As they made their plans, Jim discussed the possibility of not returning from the mission. "Well, if that's the way God wants it to be," he said, "I'm ready to die for the salvation of the Aucas." After a number of flights overhead, dropping gifts to the tribesmen, the missionaries established a beachhead across the Curaray River near the Auca village. Their objective was to continue their contact with the tribe as a prelude to communicating the gospel to them. Only days after their plane landed, the missionaries were killed and mutilated by the very ones to whom they sought to minister. Jim's death seemed almost foreshadowed in his writings. One day, after returning from an "exalting, delicious" walk to a hill, he wrote, "To gaze and glory, and to give oneself again to God, what more could a man ask? Oh the sheer excitement of knowing God on earth! I care not if I ever raise my voice again for Him, if only I may love Him, please Him."

In the eyes of the world, and of many Christians, the deaths of 29-year-old Jim Elliot and his co-workers were a waste. But that is not how they saw it. Because of their belief in the hope of heaven, they were willing to give their very lives

There are many places we put our hope, but Jesus is the only one that is secure.

Did You Know?
❓ ULTIMATE SACRIFICE

When news of the deaths of the five missionaries to the Aucas reached the outside world, the headline in the leading newspaper in Quito, the capital city of Ecuador read, "Why This Waste?" Apart from eternal values such sacrifice makes no sense, but in eternity it will matter.

for others to know of that hope. God used these men for His glory. Upon hearing the news of the tragedy, for instance, a group of Indians at a mission station in Brazil fell to their knees and cried to God for forgiveness for their own lack of concern for unsaved Indians. Remarkably, ministry to the Aucas continued and eventually two missionary women were invited to live with the tribe. Elisabeth Elliot (Jim's widowed wife) and a sister of another man killed in the attack accepted the offer and helped bring numerous Aucas to a saving knowledge of Christ. In his diary, Jim had written the following: "He is no fool who gives up what he cannot keep to gain what he cannot lose."

Jim Elliot understood his hope, and it affected how he lived. If we understand our hope, it will make a difference in how we live.

What difference does hope make?

_____

_____

_____

_____

📖 Read 1 Thessalonians 4:13–14.

What reason does Paul give for wanting them to know about their future hope?

_____

_____

_____

What would happen if they didn't understand what the Bible says about their loved ones who had died?

_____

_____

_____

_____

> *"But we do not want you to be uninformed, brethren, about those who are asleep, so that you will not grieve as do the rest who have no hope. For if we believe that Jesus died and rose again, even so God will bring with Him those who have fallen asleep in Jesus."*
>
> *1 Thessalonians 4:13-14*

Paul did not want these Christians to be uninformed about those who have *"fallen asleep"* in Jesus. Even Paul's terminology speaks the hope of the Christian message. If we believe that Jesus died and rose again, then we can have that same hope for all believers who have died. This hope is important for us to understand, for without it we would grieve like those who have no hope. Christians grieve when loved ones die, but it is not the same grief as that of the world. Ours is a grief that is mingled with hope.

📖 Look at 1 John 3:1–3. What does this passage show us will result from knowing that we will see Jesus in the future?

_____

_____

_____

If our future hope is the biblical reality that Jesus is coming back for His children and that we will spend eternity with Him, then that will affect how we live now. If our hope is *"fixed on Him,"* then we will be seeking to purify ourselves today. We will want to be ready for His return and to be found holy.

📖 Consider the message of Hebrews 6:18–19.

Is it possible that God could have misled us about our future?

_____

_____

_____

What does this hope of God's promises for the future do for our souls?

_____

_____

_____

God has promised us a glorious future. All we have to do is read the Bible and we see so many things He has promised. Yet this passage here also tells us that it is impossible for God to lie. The night before His crucifixion, Jesus told His disciples that He went to prepare a place in heaven for them. *"If it were not so,"* He explained, *"I would have told you"* (John 14:2). God would not mislead us about what awaits us in eternity. The hope of our future, these verses tell us, serves as an "anchor" for our souls. It holds on to us in the storms of life. Verse 19 calls our hope, *"both sure and steadfast."*

📖 Read 2 Corinthians 3:12. What difference does understanding our hope have on how we talk to unbelievers about Christ?

_____

_____

_____

_____

When we really understand what God has promised those who believe, it makes us bold in sharing so glorious a hope with those who don't know Him. First Peter 3:15 tells us we should always be *"ready to make a defense to everyone who asks you to give an account for the hope that is in you, yet with gentleness and reverence."*

As Christians we have a message of hope that is worth talking about. The more we understand that hope, the easier it will be to share it with others.

FOR ME TO FOLLOW GOD

Hope **DAY FIVE**

The story of Edith Burns, a parable written by the late Russell Kelfer of San Antonio, Texas, provides an excellent illustration of one who has their hope fixed on eternity. Edith Burns was a wonderful Christian who lived in San Antonio, Texas. She was the patient of a doctor

> ### "For to me, to live is Christ and to die is gain."
>
> ### Philippians 1:21

by the name of Will Phillips. Phillips was a gentle doctor who saw patients as people, and his favorite patient was Edith. One morning he went to his office with a heavy heart, and it was because of Edith Burns. When he walked into that waiting room, there sat Edith with her big black Bible in her lap earnestly talking to a young mother sitting beside her. Edith Burns had a habit of introducing herself in this way: "Hello, my name is Edith Burns. Do you believe in Easter?" Then she would explain the meaning of Easter, and many times people would be saved. After being called back in the doctor's office, Edith sat down and when she took a look at the doctor she said, "Dr. Will, why are you so sad? Are you reading your Bible? Are you praying?" Dr. Phillips said gently, "Edith, I'm the doctor and you're the patient." With a heavy heart he said, "Your lab report came back, and it says you have cancer, and Edith, you're not going to live very long." Edith said, "Why, Will Phillips, shame on you. Why are you so sad? Do you think God makes mistakes? You have just told me I'm going to see my precious Lord Jesus, my husband, and my friends. You have just told me that I am going to celebrate Easter forever, and here you are having difficulty giving me my ticket!"

Do you have such a view of your own life and death? The apostle Paul did. He wrote to the Philippian believers who were concerned about his imprisonment for the sake of the gospel, *"For to me, to live is Christ, and to die is gain"* (Philippians 1:21). He did not have this view because he was an apostle, nor did he have this view because he was so superior to you and me. He held this view of his own life and death because he understood the hope of his future with Christ. If fact, he went on to say that he had *"the desire to depart and be with Christ, for that is very much better."* But he recognized God had a purpose for his days on earth as well—to minister to others. His hope was in eternity, not in this life.

Jesus said, *"Do not lay up for yourselves treasures upon earth, where moth and rust destroy, and where thieves break in and steal. But lay up for yourselves treasures in heaven, where neither moth nor rust destroys, and where thieves do not break in or steal; for where your treasure is, there will your heart be also"* (Matthew 6:19–21). A mature focus on our hope will manifest itself in the things we treasure and what we do with our treasures.

 As you consider your own walk with the Lord, reflect on each of the following statements and rate your response.

The things I currently value most are treasures in heaven.
Mostly True   1   2   3   4   5   Mostly False

My time, finances, and affections accurately demonstrate to others my heart's conviction.
Mostly True   1   2   3   4   5   Mostly False

I'm sure that I am laying up treasures for eternity.
Mostly True   1   2   3   4   5   Mostly False

In the busyness of life in modern America, it is seldom one can make a decision that affects eternity without also making one that affects the here and now. Let me explain. Most Christians I meet, like everyone else, are very busy. Therefore if they are challenged with an opportunity of eternal benefit, saying, "Yes" to it likely means saying, "No" to something they are already doing. That is why being able to discern between things of temporal and eternal value is of so great a consequence. It grieves my heart, as I am certain it does the heart of God, to see so many well-intentioned Christians saying, "No" to things of eternal weight because they "don't have time." Yet if we observe their lives, they are already saying, "Yes" to so many things of no benefit to eternity.

APPLY It is the temporal (temporary) that often is the enemy of the eternal in our lives. As you reflect on your own spiritual life, does the Lord bring to mind any areas of your life where temporal values are supplanting eternal ones?

_____

_____

_____

_____

_____

Paul desired that the Thessalonian church be continually informed about their hope (1 Thessalonians 4:13). Would you consider yourself informed about your future hope with the Lord?

_____

_____

If not, a good place to start might be to look up in a Bible concordance (or ask your pastor or Sunday school teacher to help you) and find every time the word "hope" is used in the New Testament. Not all these verses will be relevant, but many of them will, and reading them will give you a clearer picture of what God has promised for His people.

One of the great missionaries of a century ago was a man named C. T. Studd. Mr. Studd hailed from Great Britain, and was the "Michael Jordan" of his generation and sport (cricket). Yet he turned his back on a lucrative career in professional sports to go to Africa as a missionary. On scales of temporal values, it would seem he chose foolishly, yet in light of eternity, preaching the gospel to those who had never heard was far more important to him than success in professional sports. One thing that affected him greatly, which he often quoted, was a quote he heard from an atheist:

> _If I firmly believed, as millions say they do, that the knowledge and practice of religion in this life influences destiny in another, then religion would mean to me everything. I would cast away earthly enjoyments as dross, earthly cares as follies, and earthly thought and feelings as vanity. Religion would be my first waking thought and my last image before sleep sank me into unconsciousness, I should labor in its cause alone. I would esteem one soul gained for heaven worth a life of suffering. Earthly consequences would never stay my head or seal my lips. Earth, its joys and griefs, would occupy no moment of my thoughts. I would strive to look up eternity alone, and on the immortal souls around me, soon to be everlastingly miserable. I would go forth to the world and preach to it in season and out of season. And my text would be, "WHAT SHALL IT PROFIT A MAN IF HE GAIN THE WHOLE WORLD AND LOSE HIS OWN SOUL?"_ (Norman Grubb, _C. T. Studd,_ p. 32, Fort Washington, PA, Christian Literature Crusade, 1972)

Most Christians I meet, like everyone else, are very busy. Therefore if they are challenged with an opportunity of eternal benefit, saying, "Yes" to it likely means saying, "No" to something they are already doing. That is why being able to discern between things of temporal and eternal value is of so great a consequence.

As you reflect on your Christian hope and how it affects your life today, why not write your thoughts out to the Lord as a prayer in the space provided below.

_____

_____

_____

_____

_____

_____

_____

_____

_____

_____

_____

_____

_____

_____

_____

_____

_____

_____

Notes

Notes

step eleven

Love

When the apostle Paul made his short list of the things that would last (1 Corinthians 13:13), he identified only three things: faith, hope, and love. Even within those, he identified that love was the greatest of the three. In that same passage Paul identified several things that would not last. *"Gifts of prophecy,"* Paul informed us, *"will be done away."* *"If there are tongues, they will cease; if there is knowledge, it will be done away."* Often in our spiritual lives we major on those things that are temporary instead of those that are permanent. We think maturity is reflected in the supernatural or in the super-spiritual. We think if we knew more than anyone else, or could speak the mind of God, or could speak with other languages, we would really be something. Paul makes it clear that there are more important things than those that are temporal. They may not be flashy, but the things that will last are really those things that are most important.

Over the course of these last few lessons, we have looked at faith as a practical measure of our maturity. How willing are we to trust God—to take Him at His word? We looked at hope as another measure of spiritual maturity. Do we keep in focus the future promises of God for us and do we allow that focus to affect how we live today? The final member of this triad is love,

"But now abide faith, hope, love, these three; but the greatest of these is love."

1 Corinthians 13:13

and Paul calls it the most important of the three—"the greatest." God has called us to a life of love. He has called us to be like Him. Listen to the words of the apostle John: *"Beloved, let us love one another, for love is from God; and every one who loves is born of God and knows God. The one who does not love does not know God, for God is love"* (1 John 4:7–8). God IS love. Love isn't merely something God does; it is part of who He is. We are never more like God than when we truly love.

Love **DAY ONE**

THE PRIORITY OF LOVE

There is a tendency in spiritual circles to think that others (and therefore, God) should be impressed by how much we know. Information equals godliness and spiritual value. We might not say it in those terms, but this terse message is preached loudly by how we live. Another tendency is to think that others (and therefore, God) should be impressed by how gifted and talented we are. The fact that giftedness equals importance is the unspoken message here. But neither of these messages in itself is affirmed by the Bible. In fact, it is quite the opposite. James tells us that we should prove ourselves doers of the Word and not merely hearers *"who delude themselves"* (1:22). In layman's terms, knowledge alone deludes us or deceives us into thinking we are spiritual because of how much we know instead of how we live. In 1 Corinthians 8:1, Paul wrote, *"Knowledge makes arrogant, but love edifies."* The apostle Paul spoke extensively of spiritual giftedness in 1 Corinthians 12, but he closed out the chapter by saying, *"And I show you a still more excellent way"* (verse 31), and spent the whole next chapter talking about love. Do you get the point? Love is what really matters in the Christian life.

When something is emphasized over and over as being of great importance, it is essential that we identify what it is and what it isn't. The English term "love" has been so cheapened by overuse that by it we can mean anything or nothing at all. We "love" God, but we also "love" potato chips. Yet the language of the Bible was not so careless with the term. In fact, there are four different Greek words for love. The one we speak of when we speak of God's love is the word *agape*. It describes God's unconditional commitment to us—which seeks to benefit us by doing what we need. It is selfless love, and stands in stark contrast to everything else we call love.

When Paul wrote to the Corinthian church, he wrote to a group of Christians that were out of balance. Their church services were pure chaos with everyone trying to put in their two-cents worth. They lacked no knowledge (1:5), used none of their spiritual gifts (1:7), and were far from godly. Paul was trying to re-educate them about the proper place and function of spiritual gifts, yet in the midst of this discussion, he spent an entire chapter talking about love, or as he called it, the *"more excellent way."* Let's look at what he says.

📖 Read 1 Corinthians 13:1.

What special gifts does Paul speak of here?

_____

_____

Word Study
LOVE

The Greek language had four different words for love . . .

Eros: Erotic or sensual love

Philia: Friend love or friendship

Storgē: Parental love

Agapē: Unconditional love, love of God

What is their impact without love?

_____

_____

The Corinthian church members prided themselves in their ability to speak in unknown tongues. A unique supernatural manifestation of God's power first occurred on the day of Pentecost, when travelers from other nations miraculously heard the gospel message in their native languages. Although such phenomena were repeated several times in the book of Acts, speaking in tongues was never the main emphasis of the early church. Yet it apparently had become the main emphasis in Corinth. Paul makes it clear that speaking in the tongues of other men or even in the heavenly tongue of angels is nothing more than senseless noise if it is not accompanied by love.

📖 Take a look at 1 Corinthians 13:2.

What gifts are mentioned here?

_____

_____

_____

_____

What is their result without love?

_____

_____

_____

_____

In verse 1, Paul spoke of one of the "sign" gifts—a supernatural gift that points us to God. Here in verse 2, Paul mentions several of what are known as the "foundation" gifts. These are the gifts upon which the early church was founded. The gifts of prophecy, knowledge, and faith are essential for a church to be birthed; however, a foundation built with these three gifts is structurally flawed without love. Gifts without love accomplish nothing, and Paul goes one step further to say that without love *"I am nothing."*

📖 Take a moment to consider what Paul says in 1 Corinthians 13:3.

What gifts and service are mentioned here?

_____

_____

_____

What is their result without love?

_____

_____

_____

Word Study
SENSELESS NOISE

First Corinthians 13:1 says, *"If I speak with the tongues of men and of angels, but do not have love, I have become a noisy gong or a clanging cymbal."* In the culture of Corinth, a noisy gong was usually associated with the "Copper Bowl of Dodona" at the oracle of Dodona. It was said to sound all day long and therefore was used to describe a person who talked incessantly. This cultural insight suggests that eloquence without love is not only empty noise but also annoying.

Extra Mile
HOW DOES LOVE RELATE TO SPIRITUAL GIFTS?

The subject of spiritual gifts is addressed in four different passages in the New Testament: Romans 12:3–8, I Corinthians 12:1–31, Ephesians 4:11–14 and I Peter 4:10–11. In each of these passages the subject of love is addressed in the same immediate context. Look at these verses:

- **Romans 12:9**
- **I Corinthians 13:1–13**
- **Ephesians 4:15–16**
- **I Peter 4:8–9**

Think of what Paul says here. If I give away everything I own, but my motive is anything other than love, there is no profit in it. I will not be rewarded spiritually for such actions. Even if I am a martyr, but my offering of myself is without love, my sacrifice makes no real difference. Love is superior to ministry.

Love is superior to the supernatural; it is superior to the spiritual; and it is superior to the sacrificial. Paul is not putting down gifts here, but elevating love. He is not saying knowledge is bad. We need knowledge, but not knowledge by itself. Love without knowledge is deficient, but knowledge without love is dangerous. They must both be exercised. If we call the divine abilities to serve one another "spiritual gifts," then perhaps love should be called "spiritual gift wrapping." All that we do must be wrapped in love or our service will not make a difference.

Love DAY TWO   THE PRACTICE OF LOVE

In the human mind, we tend to think of love as an emotion. We think of the great passion with which Romeo loves Juliet. While love produces very strong emotions, it is far more than just emotion—it is action. The apostle John was at first known as one of the "sons of thunder" (Mark 3:17), yet Jesus made such a difference in his life that he came to be known as the apostle of love. He referred to himself as the disciple whom Jesus loved. John was so gripped by the love of God for him that he couldn't help expressing that love toward others. He wrote, *"We love, because He first loved us"* (1 John 4:19). But again, John's love was not just emotion, but also a course of action. He also wrote, *"Little children, let us not love with word or with tongue, but in deed and truth"* (1 John 3:18). In other words, "Don't just say it, show it." John could say this because his life backed it up. As we continue looking at 1 Corinthians 13, we want to consider not just the priority of love, but the practice as well.

📖 Read through 1 Corinthians 13:4–7 slowly and reflectively. Now as you go back through it, look at the two things from verse 4 that love "is." What do you think these words mean?

Love is patient

_____

_____

_____

Love is kind

_____

_____

_____

While much practical application can be gained by thinking on the meanings of these words in English, even more can be learned from the meaning of the original Greek words. The Greek word for "patient" is *makrothuméo,* from *makro* (long) and *thumos* (wrath or anger). It means to be long or slow to get angry. It is used to communicate the idea of being patient with people, rather than with circumstances and situations. We are loving someone when we are patient with them and slow to get angry. The word "kind" is from the root word *chrestos*, which means useful or beneficial. We are loving someone when we seek to benefit them and to be useful to them.

📖 Look at 1 Corinthians 13:4–7 and identify all the things it teaches us that love **is not** or **does not do.**

_____

_____

_____

_____

_____

_____

Sometimes it is most helpful to define what a thing is by defining what it is not. Here Paul spends considerable time doing just that. He tells us first of all that love is not jealous. Jealousy or envy has the idea of comparing our lot to what someone else has. We are marked by self-centeredness if we cannot rejoice with what someone else has without wanting it for ourselves. Another thing that love is not is boastful or bragging—thinking too highly of oneself. Pride is at odds with real love, leading directly to the next negative verb Paul mentions: love is not arrogant. The Greek word for arrogant (*phusioō*) literally means "to inflate or puff up" and is used to describe a braggart or "windbag." The word figuratively portrays the idea of one who is always trying to make himself or herself out to be more than he or she is. This is a mark of one who loves self, not of one who loves others.

Love *"does not act unbecomingly."* The Greek word for "act unbecomingly" (*aschēmoneō*) literally means to behave in an ugly, indecent, unseemly or unbecoming manner. Love does not intentionally cause disgrace to another, nor does it *"seek its own"*—in other words, it does not put self first. Love *"is not provoked"*—it is not easily aroused to anger. As one quickly sees, the kind of love God calls us to have for each other is very different from the kind of sappy, valentine-like emotions that we hear of in love songs and love stories. True love, we are told here, *"does not take into account a wrong suffered."* The Greek word for "account" (*logizomai*) was used of financial reckonings. In other words, love isn't always keeping score and recording debits and credits to bring up in the future. Finally, love does not rejoice in unrighteousness. At first glance, this **"does not"** of love may seem a little out of place, until you think about it. Essentially, the point Paul makes is that love is so committed to a person's best, that it is unable—even if one cares deeply for the other—to find any joy in another's wrongdoing. To truly love someone means we are willing to point out their wrongs to them, not ignore them or join in them.

When you understand all that love is not, you begin to see how beautiful this kind of love really is. Each of us longs in the deepest recesses of our being to be loved like this. Paul says that we ought to start by showing such a love to others. How do we do that? By dealing with the "don'ts" as they show up in our lives, turning away from them toward what love calls us to do.

If we call the divine abilities to serve one another "spiritual gifts" then perhaps love should be called "spiritual gift wrapping." All that we do must be wrapped in love or our service will not make a difference.

📖 Read through 1 Corinthians 13:6b–7 and identify the positive commands of these verses.

_____

_____

_____

Word Study
LOVE IS A VERB

Love is an action, not just an emotion. As we look through these verses in 1 Corinthians 13:4–7, there are fifteen descriptive terms of what love is, and all of them are verbs. In other words, love is something you do, not just something you feel.

Love does not rejoice in unrighteousness, but rejoices in the truth. We are not loving someone when we cheer them for doing wrong. We love them when we speak truth, even if it is the truth of rebuke. Proverbs 27:5–6 tells us, *"Better is open rebuke than love that is concealed. Faithful are the wounds of a friend, but deceitful are the kisses of an enemy."* We are being loving when we speak truth for someone's good, even if it will wound him or her. As believers we can rejoice only in truth. Paul goes on in verse 7 to tell us that love *"bears all things"* (love is supportive), *"believes all things"* (love trusts that the motives of action are pure—it thinks the best of others), *"hopes all things"* (where error is seen, love hopes for change), and *"endures all things"* (bears up patiently). Love has this indefatigable capacity to endure in spite of the ingratitude, bad conduct, and problems that eventually show up in any relationship that continues long enough. Love is action—love is something we do, not just something we feel.

Love **DAY THREE**

THE PERMANENCE OF LOVE

"Till death do us part"—I've heard these words more times than I can count. You probably have too. Every wedding is marked by vows of permanent love. Yet sadly, not every marriage is permanent. Why is that? I would suggest that many marriages today are built on the shaky foundation of emotions instead of the bedrock of commitment. Now, I am no marriage expert, but I do see a lot of marriages come and go. I am a pastor, and I do my share of pre-marital counseling, wedding ceremonies, and marriage counseling. What I try to point out from the very beginning is that it is commitment that produces abiding emotions, not the other way around. Emotions are like "free agents" in the world of professional sports; in other words, they can change teams at a moment's notice. But a decision to commit can keep those emotions coming back to a place of abiding. That principle is true for marriage, and it is also true for all our relationships in the body of Christ. But most of all, it is true of God's love for us. Because we have been adopted into His family, God has made a permanent commitment to us. He will love us no matter what we do. Because God is eternal, and God is love, God's love is eternal. Gifts will end. Love will not. Therefore, our acting in love toward others should have no end either. In a world of broken promises and broken hearts, God wants His people to be marked by the permanent love that He is.

📖 Read through 1 Corinthians 13:8.

What do you think it means that love "never fails"?

_____

_____

_____

Why do you think Paul mentions the things that he says will not last?

_____

_____

_____

_____

_____

Love never fails. Is that really true? It is if you understand "agape" love. What Paul really means here is not that human love will never let us down, but that when we love with God's love, that love will always accomplish the purpose God intends. In other words, "God's love always works." Even when nothing else works, God's love still does. It is an interesting point that Paul makes here. He mentions three things that won't last. Each of them—prophecy, tongues, and knowledge—was apparently something the Corinthians thought a lot about and tried to emphasize in their church. To paraphrase, Paul says, "You are majoring on something that is temporal when you ought to be majoring on something permanent: Love."

📖 What do you think verses 9–10 mean in contrast to love?

_____

_____

_____

_____

We saw that the gifts are passing. Here Paul shows us that they are also partial. They aren't complete. They aren't enough by themselves. It seems to me that the point Paul makes is that the whole purpose of gifts is to enable us to love here and now. The gifts are a means to an end, not the end itself. But a day is coming when such tools will no longer be needed. In the presence of Christ, love will still matter but gifts won't.

📖 Why do you think Paul talks about growing up in this context (1 Corinthians 13:10–11)?

_____

_____

_____

_____

Paul seems to be saying, "We will outgrow the gifts, but not love." The gifts serve a purpose in the present, but not in heaven. The gifts that so enamored the Corinthian church were the sign gifts—those gifts that point us to Christ. In heaven, we will be in His perfect presence, and there will be no need to point to Him. Yet for eternity, love will still be relevant. Love knows none of the limitations mentioned of the gifts in these verses. The virtues listed in verses 4–7 outlast any gift and are to be cultivated earnestly.

Love is action—love is something we do, not just something we feel.

DAY FOUR # THE PRODUCT OF LOVE

When we face death, the sobering knowledge that our time on earth is fleeting tends to reduce the concerns of life to matters of most importance. Trivial matters are quickly discarded. When Jesus faced His own death, His conversations with the disciples were anything but trivial. The gospel of John devotes five chapters to all that Jesus said and did the night before His arrest and crucifixion. Over the course of that evening, three times Jesus repeated a specific command. The context of the command alone speaks of its significance. In John 13:34, Jesus said, *"A new commandment I give to you, that you love one another, even as I have loved you, that you also love one another."* In John 15:12, He repeated, *"This is My commandment, that you love one another, just as I have loved you."* And again, in John 15:17 He told them, *"This I command you, that you love one another."* By now, you should be getting the idea that love for others is something Jesus feels strongly about. Why is Jesus so concerned that we love one another? Well, for one thing, He wants us to be like God, and God is love (see 1 John 4:8, 16). Another reason is that we all need to be loved and we need not be focused only on ourselves. Christ has liberated us from being slaves of self. Ironically, God has designed life in such a way that when we focus on self, we become isolated, but when we forget self, the deepest needs of our hearts end up getting met. God wants us to be agents of love. If we are, such displays of love will have a positive impact upon the lives of others and we will be blessed well for being obedient to God's greatest commandment.

📖 Look at John 13:34–35.

What does Jesus command us to do (verse 34)?

_____

_____

_____

_____

What does He say will result if we do (verse 35)?

_____

_____

_____

_____

"Love never fails."

1 Corinthians 13:8

Jesus didn't suggest that we love one another; He commanded it. In fact, He called it a "new" commandment. The Jews were very familiar with the idea of commandments, and they were very proud of the Ten Commandments God had given to Moses on Mount Sinai. But in their zeal to obey the letter of the law, they had neglected the most important commandments: to love the Lord and to love others (Matthew 22:37–39). Jesus tells us in verse 35 that it is by our love for one another that others will see the reality of God in us. The great Christian apologist, Francis Schaeffer, called love "the final apologetic"—the final proof of Christianity. It is not our morality that convinces the unbelieving world that God is real. It is our ability to love.

📖 Read 1 Corinthians 8:1.

What is the result of knowledge?

_____

_____

_____

What is the result of love?

_____

_____

_____

Often we think, *If I knew everything, I would really be somebody.* But it is clear from this verse that knowledge alone doesn't make someone better or useful. When Paul says that knowledge *"makes arrogant"* the Greek term (*phusioō*) literally means, "knowledge puffs up." It inflates our view of ourselves. But the meaning of *phusioō* goes far deeper than that. Paul's description of human wisdom paints the picture of what today would be something like a balloon—something that looks big because it is full of air, yet has no real substance. Love, on the other hand, instead of making us arrogant, makes us useful. Love "edifies." The word means to build others up. Love always benefits others.

📖 Take a look at 1 Peter 4:8.

What are we instructed to do?

_____

_____

_____

What will result when we do this?

_____

_____

_____

_____

Love is not the only thing Peter instructs believers here to do, but it is the most important. *"Above all"* he phrases it, we are to keep fervent in our love for each other. One of the results of a life of loving is that love will make up for many offenses. Each of us makes mistakes. We are all flawed and prone to failure. Some of those mistakes will hurt others. But if our lives are characterized by *agape* love, then it will be easy for others to overlook our mistakes. Love covers a multitude of sins.

Think about what we have learned today. Love makes a difference. It makes an impact wherever it is shown. It proves to the unbeliever the reality of Christ. It builds up other believers with whom we interact, and it makes up for our own failings. No wonder the Bible makes such a big deal about love.

Did You Know?

❓ THE GREATEST COMMANDMENT

God gave Israel ten commandments written on tablets of stone and delivered to Moses. By the time of Christ, Jewish rabbis had expanded those ten commands into 642 laws the people were expected to keep. Yet Jesus said that the whole law is fulfilled in two commandments: love God with all your heart, soul, mind and strength, and love your neighbor as yourself (Matthew 22:37–40). He reduced the 642 laws of men to one word: love.

FOR ME TO FOLLOW GOD

Someone has wisely said, "People don't care how much you know until they know how much you care." One of the measures of our spiritual progress is how we do at caring. God has called us to love, and what He calls us to do, He has enabled us to do. He gives us the ability to love. The apostle John wrote, *"We love, because He first loved us"* (1 John 4:19). It is our own experience of God's love that enables to be an agent of that love to others. God's love is not like human love. He loves us not because of who and what we are, but in spite of who we are. In turn, He enables us to love, not just the lovely, but the unlovely as well. The apostle Peter wrote, *"Let all be harmonious, sympathetic, brotherly, kindhearted, and humble in spirit; not returning evil for evil, or insult for insult, but giving a blessing instead"* (1 Peter 3:8–9). How well we do at loving our neighbor says much about how far we have come in our spiritual life.

 How do you think you are doing in this area of loving others? As you consider your own behavior, where would you place yourself in comparison to others?

☐ Less loving than others
☐ About the same
☐ More loving than others

Having asked you that question, I must quickly confess that it was a trick question. In fact, I think that very question is part of our problem. You see, the measure is not how I compare to those around me. My calling is not simply to be as good or better than those around me. It is to be like Christ. The right question is not "Do I love like others?" but "Do I love like Christ would?" How would you rate yourself in that?

_____

_____

_____

I think it would be fair to say that Christ fulfilled 1 Corinthians 13. If God is love, then God in the flesh would be the model of love. If we want to be like Him, then this chapter ought to show us where we are weak. Look through the fifteen verbs below that describe love and identify the two or three you feel are most evident in your life and the two or three you feel are most lacking as well.

Love ...
Is patient
Is kind
Is not jealous
Is not a braggart
Is not arrogant
Does not act unbecomingly
Does not seek its own
Is not easily provoked
Keeps no account of wrongs suffered
Does not rejoice in unrighteousness
Rejoices in truth

Bears all things
Believes all things
Hopes all things
Endures all things

As we consider how we are doing at love, each of us, if perfectly honest, would admit to falling short. Our hearts are still marred by selfishness, and we do not love as we should. So where do we begin? If John is right, and *"We love, because He first loved us"* (1 John 4:19), then our loving others begins with our experience of God's love.

 Consider the following exercise and check the appropriate boxes next to the characteristic that best describes your current situation.

My understanding of God's forgiveness of my sins is . . .
☐ mostly head knowledge
☐ something that grips my heart

My fellowship with God is . . .
☐ real and personal
☐ rote and impersonal

My confidence that God loves me is based on . . .
☐ how I do at obeying and not sinning
☐ grace and the work of Christ

We need to be awash in the love of God. We need to be confident in His love for us, or we will not be effective at loving others. Summarize by answering the question below:

What does the way I love others say about how I think God loves me?

_____

_____

_____

_____

_____

If we are genuinely experiencing God's love, it will flow through us to others. We may know God loves us but aren't experiencing that love because of sin in our lives that affects our fellowship with God. If this is the case, our lack of experiencing God's love may be affecting how we do at loving others. If you feel this is a problem in your life, take some time to review Lesson Four on the principle of avoiding sin. God wants you to experience His love and forgiveness, and doing so will enable you to love and forgive others. In Revelation 2:4, Jesus warns the church of Ephesus that they had left their *"first love."* They were busy working hard **for** God instead of walking **with** God. He warns that the consequence of not dealing with this issue of pride and self-centeredness is that He would take away their light; in other words, God would no longer shine through them if they didn't return to their first love.

I have the **ability** to love because God loves me. I also have the **responsibility** to love. If we understand the basic teaching of the Bible, we know that we cannot save ourselves. We stand before God always and only by grace and mercy. Yet it is so easy not to be that way with others. On one hand we easily

"Above all, keep fervent in your love for one another, because love covers a multitude of sins."

1 Peter 4:8

"We love, because He first loved us."

1 John 4:19

rejoice in mercy and grace from God, yet on the other we often demand justice from each other. We expect others to treat us perfectly, and we get upset when they don't. That isn't love. God has loved us and expects us to love one another unconditionally. In fact, He commands us to love one another.

APPLY Have you recently been unloving toward anyone? If so, what steps do you need to take to go and make things right?

_____

_____

_____

_____

_____

What are some ways you can creatively express love to those around you?

_____

_____

_____

Ask God to make you sensitive to the people that make up your world. Pray for them, and ask for ways you can show them love. Everyone will recognize you as a disciple of Jesus if you love others. Why not write out a prayer that expresses this heart in the space below.

_____

_____

_____

_____

_____

_____

_____

_____

_____

_____

We stand before God always and only by grace and mercy. Yet. . . . we often demand justice from each other. We expect others to treat us perfectly, and we get upset when they don't. That isn't love.

The most important thing we are called to do as Christians is to love one another. But since true love (*agapē*) is not just an emotion, but an action, loving one another will result in many practical actions. The Bible lists a great many commands of what God calls us to do for one another. In doing them, we express love.

Each of us has experienced the pain, frustration, and resentment that comes when others fail to live up to our expectations. And yet, often our expectations of ourselves are far less than what we expect of others. Each of the verses on the following page reveals one of the responsibilities that lie on "our side of the fence," for our actions are the only ones we can control.

THE ONE ANOTHER COMMANDS

COMMAND	SCRIPTURE	COMMAND	SCRIPTURE
Not Dealing Falsely	Leviticus 19:11	Accountability	2 Corinthians 9:5
Not Wronging	Leviticus 25:14–17	Meeting Needs	2 Corinthians 11:9
Don't Rule Severely	Leviticus 25:46	Serving Through Love	Galatians 5:13
Pray	1 Samuel 12:23a	Do Not Bite and Devour	Galatians 5:15
Dwell in Unity	Psalm 133:1	Do Not Challenge	Galatians 5:26b
Love at all times	Proverbs 17:17a	Do Not Envy	Galatians 5:26c
Faithful Wounds	Proverbs 27:5–6	Bear Burdens	Galatians 6:2
Sharpen	Proverbs 27:17	Do Good	Galatians 6:10
Lift up	Ecclesiastes 4:9–10	Showing Forbearance	Ephesians 4:2
Do Not Devise Evil	Zechariah 7:10	Speak Truth	Ephesians 4:25
Speak the Truth	Zechariah 8:16	Give, Don't Take	Ephesians 4:27
Be at Peace	Mark 9:50	Be Kind	Ephesians 4:32
Do not seek Glory from Man	John 5:44	Forgive	Ephesians 4:32
Love	John 13:34–35	Be Subject	Ephesians 5:21
Lay Down Your Self	John 15:12–17	Regard Others More Important	Philippians 2:3
Reconcile	Acts 7:26	Do Not Lie	Colossians 3:9
Meet Needs	Acts 11:29	Bearing With	Colossians 3:13
Bring Joy	Acts 15:3	Teaching and Admonishing	Colossians 3:16
Strengthen	Acts 15:32	Abound in Love	1 Thessalonians 3:12
Proclaim the Word	Acts 15:36	Excel in Love	1 Thessalonians 4:9–10
Encourage	Acts 16:40; 18:27	Comfort	1 Thessalonians 4:18
Be Devoted	Romans 12:10a	Encourage and Build Up	1 Thessalonians 5:11
Give Preference	Romans 12:10b	Appreciate and Esteem	1 Thessalonians 5:12–13
Be of One Mind	Romans 12:16	Do Not Repay with Evil	1 Thessalonians 5:15a
Owe Nothing But Love	Romans 13:8	Seek Good	1 Thessalonians 5:15b
Judge Not	Romans 14:13	Give Thanks	2 Thessalonians 1:3
Build Up	Romans 14:19	Point Out	1 Timothy 4:6
Bear Weakness	Romans 15:1–2	No Longer Hateful	Titus 3:1–4
Glorify Together	Romans 15:5–6	Encourage	Hebrews 3:13
Accept One Another	Romans 15:7	Stimulate to Love & Good Deeds	Hebrews 10:24
Admonish	Romans 15:14	Assemble to Encourage	Hebrews 10:25
Do Not Sue	1 Corinthians 6:1–8	Love and Hospitality	Hebrews 13:1–3
Stop Depriving	1 Corinthians 7:5	Visit Widows and Orphans	James 1:27
No Cause for Stumbling	1 Corinthians 8:12	Speak Not Against	James 4:11
Wait	1 Corinthians 11:33	Do Not Complain Against	James 5:9
No Division	1 Corinthians 12:25	Confess	James 5:16a
Respect	1 Corinthians 16:11	Pray	James 5:16b

THE ONE ANOTHER COMMANDS
(CONTINUED)

COMMAND	SCRIPTURE	COMMAND	SCRIPTURE
Love From the Heart	1 Peter 1:22	Laying Down our Lives	1 John 3:14–16
Give a Blessing	1 Peter 3:8–9a	Love in Deed	1 John 3:17–18
Love Fervently	1 Peter 4:8	Believe = Love	1 John 3:23
Hospitality Without Complaint	1 Peter 4:9	Love One Another	1 John 4:7–21
Serve	1 Peter 4:10	Love = Obedience	2 John 1:5
Humility	1 Peter 5:5	Doing for the Brethren	3 John 1:5–6
Walk in the Light	1 John 1:7	Becoming Fellow Workers	3 John 1:7–8
Righteous Love	1 John 3:10–11	Do Good to the Brethren	3 John 1:10–11

Notes

Notes

step twelve

Stewardship

What will you say about your accomplishments at the end of your life? That is a most challenging question. Hugo Grotius, the father of modern international law, said at the last, "I have accomplished nothing worthwhile in my life." John Quincy Adams, sixth President of the United States wrote in his diary: "My life has been spent in vain and idle aspirations, and in ceaseless rejected prayers that something would be the result of my existence beneficial to my species." Robert Louis Stevenson wrote words that continue to delight and enrich our lives, and yet what did he pen for his epitaph? "Here lies one who meant well, who tried a little, and failed much." Cecil Rhodes opened up Africa and established an empire, but what were his dying words? "So little done, so much to do." At the end of our lives the burning questions will not be concerned with what opportunities and abilities were given to us, but with what we did with those opportunities and abilities.

Jesus' last words as He hung on the cross, dying, were *"It is finished!"* His earthly life was a life that accomplished its purpose. The apostle Paul, at the end of his life wrote, *"I have fought the good fight, I have finished the course, I have kept the faith"* (2 Timothy 4:7). In other words, He had done what God had for Him to do. Each one of us will come to the end of our days, and will stand before the Lord to give an answer for how we lived them. Our labors will not be compared to what others have done, but to what we could and should have done. God wants to reward us for our faithfulness.

In Matthew 25:14–30 Jesus was addressing the "last days," and in that context He told what is called "The Parable of the Talents." In this parable, He tells of a master who goes on a journey and entrusts his possessions to three servants. To one he gave five talents, to another two, and to the last one he gave one talent. The distribution was to each *"according to his own ability."* The first two servants took the talents entrusted to them and traded with them, doubling their master's money. But the third servant buried his one talent, doing nothing with it. When the master returned, his response to the first two servants was, *"Well done, good and faithful slave,"* and greater responsibilities were given to them. But to the third who had been unfaithful, what he had was taken away and given to the first. Like those servants, each of us has been entrusted with responsibilities to manage. Like them, we each await our Master's return, and when He does, faithfulness will be rewarded. In this lesson we want to look at those things God has made us stewards of as Christians, for we want to be found faithful when He returns.

If we are called to be stewards, and if one day we will give an account to God for our stewardship, then we need to know over what things we are to be a steward. The Scriptures spell out four precious commodities that must be managed prudently. In this lesson we want to consider these four.

Stewardship **DAY ONE**

STEWARDSHIP OF TIME

"Therefore be careful how you walk, not as unwise men, but as wise, making the most of your time, because the days are evil."

Ephesians 5:15–16

When I was in college, I was not the most astute manager of time. I generally got my work done on schedule, but I also wasted a lot of time watching television and hanging out with my friends. One day, however, I had so wasted my time that I didn't complete an assigned term paper when it was due. I went to the professor to request an extension, and when he asked why, I replied that I didn't have enough time. "Nonsense," the professor exclaimed. "The president of the United States has no more time in his week than you do, and he gets infinitely more work done. The issue is not if you had enough time, but what did you do with the time you had." For turning my paper in late, I was docked a letter grade from what I would have received. It was a painful lesson, but a valuable one. I have often remembered his words when I felt I didn't have enough time to do something.

Each of us operates with the same calendar, the same clock. All our minutes have sixty seconds, and every hour has sixty minutes. Your days are no longer or shorter than mine, and we are all bound to the same calendar. The only difference among any of us is how many pages on that calendar are turned before we meet our Maker. If we believe that God has a plan and a purpose for each of our lives, then we must trust that we have been allotted enough days for that purpose. But what will we do with those days?

📖 Read Ephesians 5:15–16.

What is the call of these verses?

_____

_____

What are the two possibilities mentioned?

_____

_____

_____

What is the reason given for the challenge?

_____

_____

_____

_____

Ephesians 5:15–16 exhorts us, *"Therefore be careful how you walk, not as unwise men, but as wise, making the most of your time, because the days are evil."* We are called to be careful. There is in each day, and even each hour, the potential of being wise or of being unwise. The challenge to make the most of our time is given because the days are evil. In other words, if unplanned, time does not tend to move in the direction of godliness.

Time is a perishable commodity; it is not eternal. Once used, it is gone forever, leaving in its place whatever I traded it for. A good evaluation question is "Was it worth it?" Was my use of that time worth what I have to show for it?

📖 Now look at Ephesians 5:17. What does it indicate as a key for making the most of my time?

_____

_____

_____

If I am to make the most of my time, then I need to seek God. Since the Lord knows everything about the future, He is the best one to plan my life. I need to seek His will as a habit, for His will for me will always make the most of the time He has given me. This passage goes on to indicate that a key to knowing God's will for my use of time is being "filled with the Spirit"—a concept we looked at in earlier chapters. God in control of our hearts will be able to give us the discernment we need when making choices of how to manage our time. Remember, good time management isn't just about activity, but productivity. We can be very busy (possibly too busy) and still not be in God's will. The key is whether or not we are busy doing the things we ought to be doing with our time.

📖 Consider Psalm 127:2. What does this passage teach us about time management?

_____

_____

_____

> *"So teach us to number our days, that we may present to Thee a heart of wisdom."*
>
> *Psalm 90:12*

The principle of time management can either serve us or enslave us. We need to realize that it's not so important how much we do with our time, but whether we do the right things. Sometimes the most spiritual thing you can do is go to bed and get a good night's sleep. Sleeping is a God-given need and isn't a waste of time. Taking a vacation or a day off is not unspiritual. In fact, the lack of doing so may be the most unspiritual thing we can do with our time. Psalm 127 teaches us that it is vanity to think that we can get ahead by striving and by working long hours without rest. We are not to live as machines. Walking in God's will means that we make our hours count, not that we work long hours. God's will sometimes means time with the family, not more time at work. The key here in Psalm 127 is balance. For example, I can't use stewardship as an excuse for not sleeping or not spending time with my family. I must balance my priorities.

STEWARDSHIP OF TALENTS

Every person has certain God-given abilities, both natural and spiritual, that make him unique, and God desires that those abilities be used to the fullest. Several years ago a young man asked my advice on what he should do when he graduated from college. He had some job prospects, but he was also a world-class distance runner and could make a living for a while doing that. As I helped him through the process of making the decision, I reminded him of this issue of stewardship of talents. While stewardship alone didn't guarantee that it was God's will for him to continue running, it certainly was a major factor to consider. Few of us can lay claim to being a world-class anything, much less a world-class athlete. I encouraged him to consider the tremendous platform for ministry which athletics bring and to ask God if that might be His will for now. His business degree could be picked up later, but his running couldn't. While *The Declaration of Independence* states "that all men are created equal," that is only true as far as the writers of that document intended. It goes on to state how we are equal—we "are endowed by [our] Creator with certain unalienable rights . . . Life, Liberty, and the pursuit of Happiness." But God has not created us all with equal skills, talents, and abilities. I did not come from the womb with the same potential for basketball prowess as Shaquille O'Neal. Regardless of how much effort I put into developing my gifts and abilities, I could never be effective as a center for the Los Angeles Lakers.

📖 Look at 1 Peter 4:10–11.

What do these verses say is true of every believer?

_____

_____

_____

What are we to do with our spiritual gifts?

_____

_____

_____

"As each one has received a special gift, employ it in serving one another, as good stewards of the manifold grace of God."

1 Peter 4:10

Who is to benefit from them?

_____

_____

_____

_____

Certainly natural abilities such as athletic prowess or artistic giftedness are resources to be managed, but not all of us have significant talents in these areas. Scripture teaches, however, that every believer does have spiritually endowed abilities over which God calls him to be a steward. The Bible refers to these as "spiritual gifts." We looked pretty thoroughly at the concept of spiritual gifts in Lesson 8, Day 2. In 1 Peter 4:10 we are told, *"As each one has received a special gift, employ it in serving one another, as good stewards of the manifold grace of God."* While this verse is speaking of managing our spiritual gifts, the principle can be expanded far beyond that limited scope. Anything we are good at is a blessing from God and something to be managed as a good steward. Gifts (and talents) are not simply to be used for selfish benefit.

My church is fairly large, and one of the practical needs that arise from time to time is that we need to paint our parking lot lines. As far as I know, we have never paid to have this service done. Why? Because one of our members does that as a business. He has the equipment and the ability, and he donates that service to the church. He doesn't get a contribution credit from the IRS, but he does have the satisfaction of knowing that he is a good steward of that unique ability and the equipment he is blessed to own.

📖 What are we to do with our abilities? Look up the verses below and write what you learn in them about good stewardship of our talents.

1 Timothy 4:14–15

_____

_____

_____

_____

2 Timothy 1:6

_____

_____

_____

_____

 **Word Study**
"KINDLE AFRESH"

The Greek word translated *"kindle afresh"* in 2 Timothy 1:6 (*anazōpureō*) paints a picture culturally of stirring up smoldering embers into a living flame. In the ancient world, a fire was not always kept at a continual blaze, but rather, kept alive through glowing coals that were then rekindled to a flame as needed through the use of bellows. Paul is telling Timothy, "Fan the coals of your gifts into a full flame."

From these exhortations of the apostle Paul to his disciple Timothy, we learn some important truths about stewardship of talents. First Timothy 4:14 tells us the gifts and abilities we have can be neglected. While this verse looks at the idea from the negative, the next verse as well as 2 Timothy 1:6 makes it clear that our gifts can be developed. Paul speaks in 1 Timothy 4:15 of *"taking pains"* and *"being absorbed"* with our giftedness so that others can see progress. In his second letter to Timothy, Paul reminds him to *"kindle afresh"* the gifts he has. In other words, "Don't neglect your gifts, but develop them." I think that an important component of success in life is figuring out what you are good at and then developing that area to the fullest.

📖 Read Ecclesiastes 9:10 and consider what it says about how we should manage our talents.

_____

_____

_____

God decides what abilities we have, but we decide what we will do with them.

Solomon was history's wisest king; therefore, his advice ought to be worth something. He instructs us, *"Whatever your hand finds to do, verily, do it with all your might."* Along with our talents will come God-given opportunities to use them. Solomon essentially says, "Whatever you find yourself doing, make sure you do it the best you can." Part of stewardship of our talents is a simple commitment to excellence. Anything worth doing is worth doing as well as we can. Some of the greatest works of art and music in history resulted from believers such as Michelangelo and Beethoven, who believed their talents came from God and sought to honor Him in their use of them.

Maybe you are no artist or athlete. Maybe you consider your talents to be insignificant. Perhaps they aren't as significant as someone else's, but they can still have a significant impact. The Book of Acts describes the mighty exploits of the apostle Peter, who actually raised a woman named Dorcas from the dead (Acts 9:40–41). But it also tells us that Dorcas, although she had no great supernatural power, was good at sewing. It describes her as *"abounding with deeds of kindness and charity, which she continually did"* (Acts 9:36). When she died, the widows wept over her and showed off the tunics and garments she used to make. Think about that. She used her ability for the Lord's service and was a blessing to needy widows. While Peter's raising her from the dead was certainly a miracle, it was also significant that her not-so-miraculous abilities resulted in blessings to others. Maybe that is one of the reasons God added years to her life. We can't all be Peters, but any of us can be a Dorcas when you consider that every Christian can and should be a blessing to others. God decides what abilities we have, but we decide what we will do with them.

Stewardship **DAY THREE**

STEWARDSHIP OF TREASURES

Recently, the national news media made much ado about a multi-state lottery game called "The Big Game" that saw its jackpot balloon to upwards of 325 million dollars! Since I live only a few miles from Georgia, one of the states where this lottery game is available, our local TV news was filled with images of people standing in long lines to purchase their tickets in hopes of striking it rich. While I had no intention of buying a ticket, I did reflect on what winning such a large amount of money would entail. History has shown that lottery winners do experience their lives being changed; but more often than not, the change is not for the better. If I suddenly won the lottery, what would I do with all that money? Would I give lots to charity? Hopefully. Would I spend it all wisely? Probably not. Would it change me? Definitely. For example, would I still work if I didn't need to, or would I just take a long vacation and entertain myself. Would I take the time to write a Bible study like the one you hold in your hands?

While I most likely will never become a millionaire, I do manage an estate that is perhaps worth millions. You see, over the course of my lifetime I will probably earn nearly a million dollars if not more. So will you. What we do with what we have is probably what we would do if we had more.

📖 Look at Luke 16:10–12. What does it teach us about how we would handle our money if we had more of it?

_____

_____

_____

_____

The issue of treasure isn't how much we have, but what we will do with what we have. Jesus said, *"He who is faithful in a very little thing is faithful also in much; and he who is unrighteous in a very little thing is unrighteous also in much"* (Luke 16:10). What we do with what limited treasures we presently have is probably what we would do if we had more. Stewardship of our finances says a lot regarding our spirituality. If perchance I could see your checkbook, in a few minutes I could probably tell you what your priorities and values are. The implication of Luke 16:10 is that the way we use money has something to do with what spiritual blessings God can entrust to us.

📖 Read 1 Timothy 6:17–19.

What are the dangers of being blessed financially (verse 17)?

_____

_____

_____

What should we do with our financial blessings (verse 18)?

_____

_____

_____

What does verse 19 tell us about what we can do with money?

_____

_____

_____

One of the dangers of prosperity is pride. If God blesses us, we are at risk of becoming conceited and thinking our prosperity is something we have earned or deserve. Another danger of prosperity is that our wealth becomes our hope instead of God being our hope. What should we do with our financial blessings? Well, the end of verse 17 makes it clear that it isn't wrong to enjoy them. But verse 18 goes on to instruct us that they aren't for us only. We should be generous with our blessings and use them to bless others. Verse 19 presents an interesting thought. It suggests that how we use the non-eternal commodity of money can have an eternal effect. How we use our blessings can produce eternal reward, and being quick to bless others helps us to understand that life is really about giving, not taking.

> *"He who is faithful in a very little thing is faithful also in much; and he who is unrighteous in a very little thing is unrighteous also in much."*
>
> *Luke 16:10*

> **"But who am I and who are my people that we should be able to offer as generously as this? For all things come from Thee, and from Thy hand we have given Thee."**
>
> **1 Chronicles 29:14**

📖 Look up these verses and write what they teach about who owns what.

1 Chronicles 29:11–16

_____

_____

_____

2 Corinthians 5:14–15

_____

_____

_____

We see here in 1 Chronicles that everything in the heavens and earth belongs to God. Even when we give to God, we are only giving back out of what He has already given to us. Not only does everything we have belong to God because He made us, but we are doubly His. As 2 Corinthians 5 points out, we have been bought by the blood of Christ. He didn't die for us so we could live selfish, greedy lives. He died for us so that we could live for Him as stewards of His blessings.

Stewardship of our treasures isn't really about how much we possess, but about what actually possesses us. Almost everyone can be considered rich if compared to the right person, whether locally or in another part of the world. God blesses us so we can be a blessing.

Stewardship DAY FOUR

STEWARDSHIP OF TRUTH

When I first became a Christian, at the urging of the fellow who led me to the Lord, I got involved in a Bible study a friend of his was leading. It was a six-week study of the basics of the Christian life. At the end of it, that was about all I knew of the Bible. As I shared in an earlier chapter, my teen years were marked with rebellion and immersion in the drug culture. When I became a Christian, most of my friends were still in that same lifestyle. None were Christians or even churchgoers that I knew of. As a result of seeing the changes in me, many of them became open to receiving Christ. Over those first few months the ripple affect of my changed life began to reach others. My roommate gave his life to the Lord. Two guys across the hall in our dorm became Christians. A fellow student from my hometown recommitted to his faith. The guy in the dorm room next door to me trusted Christ as well.

Suddenly I had all these guys looking to me for spiritual answers, and I didn't know much more than they did. But I had gone through that Bible study on the basics. At their request, I started a Bible study in our dorm going through that booklet I had just been through myself. None of us knew Philippians from Philistines. Every week they had questions, and just about every week I gave the same answer: "I'm not sure, but I'll find out for next week." By the end of that spring, there were fifteen guys cramming into my dorm room each week to study the Bible. I trust they learned some things, but I know I learned more than anyone.

The fourth dimension of stewardship is an area that is often omitted in sermons on the subject. Most of us have given little thought to this, but God calls every believer to be a good steward of **truth.** Perhaps the greatest lesson I learned from that dorm Bible study experience is that we are stewards of whatever God has taught us. The truth He puts in us isn't just for us. There are others around us that can benefit from it. Maybe you don't have the opportunity to lead a Bible study of new Christians, but someone around you probably needs something you have learned through this study we are doing together. Be open to sharing what you learn, and you will be surprised by how God will use you.

📖 Read Proverbs 27:17. What does it tell us about how we can be used in the lives of others?

_____

_____

_____

_____

_____

Just like iron can be used to sharpen iron, God can use us in each other's lives. You don't have to be an experienced teacher to teach things to others. If you walk in relationship with others, God will give you opportunities to share what He has taught you, and you will be surprised how much others can be blessed by that.

📖 Look at 2 Timothy 2:2.

What is the treasure Paul is calling Timothy to manage wisely?

_____

_____

_____

Who is the kind of person Timothy is to invest the truths he has been entrusted?

_____

_____

_____

God, through His servants, has invested truth in every believer. Perhaps some of us know more than others, but all of us have received some truth, and 2 Timothy 2:2 speaks loudly to this issue as Paul exhorts Timothy: *"The things which you have heard from me . . . these entrust to faithful men, who will be able to teach others also."*

Each of us has seen truth modeled and heard it taught. This truth thus becomes in our lives a treasure to be managed, a stewardship to be entrusted to others who will then do the same with still others—and the Christian faith grows and spreads. This directive is echoed in the Great Commission recorded in Matthew 28:18–20. Christ commands us to be *"teaching them to observe all that I commanded you."*

God calls every believer to be a good steward of truth.

FOR ME TO FOLLOW GOD

Every one of us is a steward of some kind. We may be good ones or bad ones, but either way we are stewards. Because God has entrusted some of His blessings to us, He has made us stewards, and He calls us to faithful management of the things that belong to Him. Maybe this is a new idea for you. Or maybe it is an idea that has expanded in your understanding through this week's lesson. Remember, you are accountable for this knowledge.

📖 Take a look at 1 Corinthians 4:1–2. What is of utmost importance for a steward?

_____

_____

_____

_____

Word Study
ENTRUST

In 2 Timothy 2:2, Paul calls us to "entrust" truth. The Greek word that is translated "entrust" is *paratithēmi* (pa-ra-tih'-thay-mee), which means to place alongside or present (as in presenting food or truth). The word can also describe the act of depositing (as trust or for protection).

Paul identifies those who would be servants of Christ as "stewards." The idea is that of one who manages the resources of another. What is expected of a steward is not perfection, but faithfulness. As we look at our own lives, faithfulness must be what we evaluate.

APPLY As you consider the different areas of stewardship, evaluate how you think you are doing in each area.

Stewardship of your time

Faithful ⟵ 1   2   3   4   5 ⟶ Unfaithful

Stewardship of your talents

Faithful ⟵ 1   2   3   4   5 ⟶ Unfaithful

Stewardship of your treasures

Faithful ⟵ 1   2   3   4   5 ⟶ Unfaithful

Stewardship of your truth

Faithful ⟵ 1   2   3   4   5 ⟶ Unfaithful

> *"In this case, moreover, it is required of stewards that one be found trustworthy."*
>
> *1 Corinthians 4:2*

APPLY As you seek the Lord about what you might need to be doing differently, let the questions below help you.

Stewardship of time:
What are the biggest areas in which you are tempted to waste time?

_____

_____

_____

_____

_____

_____

_____

Do you struggle with trusting God with getting things done, or do you strive and spend long hours on one area while neglecting others?

_____

_____

_____

_____

Stewardship of talents:
What are some of the unique gifts and abilities God has given you?

_____

_____

_____

Are there any things you can do to develop those gifts?

_____

_____

_____

Can you think of some ways you can use your talents to be a blessing to others?

_____

_____

_____

_____

Stewardship of treasures:
Have you developed a habit of giving regularly to the Lord's work?

_____

_____

_____

Giving is important on several levels. Obviously there are many ministries that need to be funded. It starts with our local churches, and spreads to the taking of the gospel to the world. But, while these causes need funds, we need to give more than anyone actually needs our money. Giving is an issue of faith. If we trust God to meet our needs, then we don't hoard our resources, but are free to share them. Giving is also a need to keep us from becoming greedy and selfish. *For where your treasure is, there will your heart be also.* Giving helps to keep our hearts from being preoccupied only with ourselves.

Here are four areas you ought to consider when determining where to give your treasure:

1) To your local church: the place that shepherds you in the faith ought to be supported financially (Galatians 6:6; 1 Timothy 5:17–18).

2) Other ministries that feed you spiritually: those who minister spiritual things to you ought to be supported (1 Corinthians 9:7–14).

3) The poor and needy: God promises that he who gives to the poor, lends to the Lord, and God will repay (2 Corinthians 8:14; 1 John 3:17).

4) Those who take the gospel to unbelievers: Missionaries can't go unless they are sent (Romans 10:14–15; 3 John 1:5–8).

Are you taking good care of your material blessings?

_____

_____

_____

_____

Stewardship of truth:
What parts of this study have ministered to you the most?

_____

_____

_____

_____

_____

Who is someone who would benefit from something you have learned from this study?

_____

_____

_____

_____

_____

How and when can you share with this person?

_____

_____

_____

_____

_____

_____

_____

_____

Each of us is a steward; that is already settled. The question of the Christian life, then, is "What kind of steward am I?" As you close out this week's lesson, write out a prayer to the Lord concerning this area of stewardship. Confess any areas of which you need to repent. Thank the Lord for what you have. Ask for His wisdom in how to be the best steward you can be of what He has trusted to you.

_____

_____

_____

_____

_____

_____

_____

_____

_____

_____

_____

_____

Each of us is a steward; that is already settled. The question of the Christian life, then, is "What kind of steward am I?"

Notes

How to Follow God

STARTING THE JOURNEY

Did you know that you have been on God's heart and mind for a long, long time? Even before time existed you were on His mind. He has always wanted you to know Him in a personal, purposeful relationship. He has a purpose for your life and it is founded upon His great love for you. You can be assured it is a good purpose and it lasts forever. Our time on this earth is only the beginning. God has a grand design that goes back into eternity past and reaches into eternity future. What is that design?

The Scriptures are clear about God's design for man—God created man to live and walk in oneness with Himself. Oneness with God means being in a relationship that is totally unselfish, totally satisfying, totally secure, righteous and pure in every way. That's what we were created for. If we walked in that kind of relationship with God we would glorify Him and bring pleasure to Him. Life would be right! Man was meant to live that way—pleasing to God and glorifying Him (giving a true estimate of who God is). Adam sinned and shattered his oneness with God. Ever since, man has come short of the glory of God: man does not and cannot please God or give a true estimate of God. Life is not right until a person is right with God. That is very clear as we look at the many people who walked across the pages of Scripture, both Old and New Testaments.

JESUS CHRIST came as the solution for this dilemma. Jesus Christ is the glory of God—the true estimate of who God is in every way. He pleased His Father in everything He did and said, and He came to restore oneness with God. He came to give man His power and grace to walk in oneness with God, to follow Him day by day enjoying the relationship for which he was created. In the process, man could begin to present a true picture of Who God is and experience knowing Him personally. You may be asking, "How do these facts impact my life today? How does this become real to me now? How can I begin the journey of following God in this way?" To come to know God personally means you must choose to receive Jesus Christ as your personal Savior and Lord.

- First of all, you must admit that you have sinned, that you are not walking in oneness with God, not pleasing Him or glorifying Him in your life (Romans 3:23; 6:23; 8:5–8).

- It means repenting of that sin—changing your mind, turning to God and turning away from sin—and by faith receiving His forgiveness based on His death on the Cross for you (Romans 3:21–26; 1 Peter 3:18).

- It means opening your life to receive Him as your living, resurrected Lord and Savior (John 1:12). He has promised to come and indwell you by His Spirit and live in you as the Savior and Master of your life (John 14:16–21; Romans 14:7–9).

- He wants to live His life through you—conforming you to His image, bearing His fruit through you and giving you power to reign in life (John 15:1,4–8; Romans 5:17; 7:4; 8:29, 37).

You can come to Him now. In your own words, simply tell Him you want to know Him personally and you willingly repent of your sin and receive His forgiveness and His life. Tell Him you want to follow Him forever (Romans 10:9–10, 13). Welcome to the family of God and to the greatest journey of all!!!

WALKING ON THE JOURNEY

How do we follow Him day by day? Remember, Christ has given those who believe in Him everything pertaining to life and godliness, so that we no longer have to be slaves to our "flesh" and its corruption (2 Peter 1:3–4). Day by day He wants to empower us to live a life of love and joy, pleasing to Him and rewarding to us. That's why Ephesians 5:18 tells us to *be filled with the Spirit*—keep on being controlled by the Spirit who lives in you. He knows exactly what we need each day and we can trust Him to lead us (Proverbs 3:5–6). So how can we cooperate with Him in this journey together?

To walk with Him *day by day* means. . .

- reading and listening to His Word day by day (Luke 10:39, 42; Colossians 3:16; Psalm 19:7–14; 119:9).

- spending time talking to Him in prayer (Philippians 4:6–7).

- realizing that God is God and you are not, and the role that means He has in your life.

This allows Him to work through your life as you fellowship, worship, pray and learn with other believers (Acts 2:42), and serve in the good works He has prepared for us to do—telling others who Jesus is and what His Word says, teaching and encouraging others, giving to help meet needs, helping others, and so forth (Ephesians 2:10).

God's goal for each of us is that we be conformed to the image of His Son, Jesus Christ (Romans 8:29). But none of us will reach that goal of perfection until we are with Him in Heaven, for then "we shall be like Him, because we shall see Him just as He is" (1 John 3:2). For now, He wants us to follow

Him faithfully, learning more each day. Every turn in the road, every trial and every blessing, is designed to bring us to a new depth of surrender to the Lord and His ways. He not only wants us to do His will, He desires that we surrender to His will His way. That takes trust—trust in His character, His plan and His goals (Proverbs 3:5–6).

As you continue this journey, and perhaps you've been following Him for a while, you must continue to listen carefully and follow closely. We never graduate from that. That sensitivity to God takes moment by moment surrender, dying to the impulses of our flesh to go our own way, saying no to the temptations of Satan to doubt God and His Word, and refusing the lures of the world to be unfaithful to the Lord who gave His life for us.

God desires that each of us comes to maturity as sons and daughters: to that point where we are fully satisfied in Him and His ways, fully secure in His sovereign love, and walking in the full measure of His purity and holiness. If we are to clearly present the image of Christ for all to see, it will take daily surrender and daily seeking to follow Him wherever He leads, however He gets there (Luke 9:23–25). It's a faithful walk of trust through time into eternity. And it is worth everything. Trust Him. Listen carefully. Follow closely.

READ THROUGH THE NEW TESTAMENT IN 90 DAYS

DAY	SCRIPTURE	DAY	SCRIPTURE
Day 1	Matt. 1:1–3:17	Day 46	1 Cor. 10:1–13:13
Day 2	Matt. 4:1–6:34	Day 47	1 Cor. 14:1–16:24
Day 3	Matt. 7:1–10:42	Day 48	2 Cor. 1:1–4:18
Day 4	Matt. 11:1–13:58	Day 49	2 Cor. 5:1–7:16
Day 5	Matt. 14:1–16:28	Day 50	2 Cor. 8:1–10:18
Day 6	Matt. 17:1–19:30	Day 51	2 Cor. 11:1–13:14
Day 7	Matt. 20:1–22:46	Day 52	Gal. 1:1–3:29
Day 8	Matt. 23:1–25:46	Day 53	Gal. 4:1–6:18
Day 9	Matt. 26:1–28:20	Day 54	Eph. 1:1–3:21
Day 10	Mark 1:1–3:35	Day 55	Eph. 4:1–6:24
Day 11	Mark 4:1–6:56	Day 56	Phil. 1:1–4:23
Day 12	Mark 7:1–9:50	Day 57	Col.1:1–4:18
Day 13	Mark 10:1–12:44	Day 58	1 Thess. 1:1–3:13
Day 14	Mark 13:1–16:20	Day 59	1 Thess. 4:1–2 Thess. 3:18
Day 15	Luke 1:1–2:52	Day 60	1 Tim. 1:1–3:16
Day 16	Luke 3:1–5:39	Day 61	1 Tim. 4:1–6:21
Day 17	Luke 6:1–8:56	Day 62	2 Tim. 1:1–4:22
Day 18	Luke 9:1–11:54	Day 63	Titus 1:1–3:15
Day 19	Luke 12:1–14:35	Day 64	Phile. 1:1–25
Day 20	Luke 15:1–17:37	Day 65	Heb. 1:1–3:19
Day 21	Luke 18:1–21:38	Day 66	Heb. 4:1–6:20
Day 22	Luke 22:1–24:53	Day 67	Heb. 7:1–9:28
Day 23	John 1:1–3:36	Day 68	Heb. 10:1–11:40
Day 24	John 4:1–6:71	Day 69	Heb. 12:1–13:25
Day 25	John 7:1–9:41	Day 70	James 1:1–3:18
Day 26	John 10:1–12:50	Day 71	James 4:1–5:20
Day 27	John 13:1–16:33	Day 72	1 Pet. 1:1–2:25
Day 28	John 17:1–19:42	Day 73	1 Pet. 3:1–5:14
Day 29	John 20:1–21:25	Day 74	2 Pet. 1:1–3:18
Day 30	Acts 1:1–3:26	Day 75	1 John 1:1–2:29
Day 31	Acts 4:1–6:15	Day 76	1 John 3:1–4:21
Day 32	Acts 7:1–9:43	Day 77	1 John 5:1–2 John 1:13
Day 33	Acts 10:1–12:25	Day 78	3 John 1:1–Jude 1:25
Day 34	Acts 13:1–15:41	Day 79	Rev. 1:1–20
Day 35	Acts 16:1–18:28	Day 80	Rev. 2:1–29
Day 36	Acts 19:1–21:40	Day 81	Rev. 3:1–22
Day 37	Acts 22:1–24:27	Day 82	Rev. 4:1–5:14
Day 38	Acts 25:1–28:31	Day 83	Rev. 6:1–7:17
Day 39	Rom. 1:1–3:31	Day 84	Rev. 8:1–9:21
Day 40	Rom. 4:1–6:23	Day 85	Rev. 10:1–11:19
Day 41	Rom. 7:1–9:33	Day 86	Rev. 12:1–13:18
Day 42	Rom. 10:1–13:14	Day 87	Rev. 14:1–16:21
Day 43	Rom. 14:1–16:27	Day 88	Rev. 17:1–18:24
Day 44	1 Cor. 1:1–4:21	Day 89	Rev. 19:1–20:15
Day 45	1 Cor. 5:1–9:27	Day 90	Rev. 21:1–22:21

The *Following God*
Bible Character Study Series

Life Principles from the Old Testament

Characters include: Adam, Noah, Job, Abraham, Lot, Jacob, Joseph, Moses, Caleb, Joshua, Gideon, and Samson
ISBN 0-89957-300-2   208 pages

Life Principles from the Kings of the Old Testament

Characters include: Saul, David, Solomon, Jereboam I, Asa, Ahab, Jehoshaphat, Hezekiah, Josiah, Zerubbabel & Ezra, Nehemiah, and "The True King in Israel."
ISBN 0-89957-301-0   256 pages

Life Principles from the Prophets of the Old Testament

Characters include: Samuel, Elijah, Elisha, Jonah, Hosea, Isaiah, Micah, Jeremiah, Habakkuk, Daniel, Haggai, and "Christ the Prophet."
ISBN 0-89957-303-7   224 pages

Leader's Guides for Following God™ books are available.
To order now, call (800) 266-4977 or (423) 894-6060.

The *Following God*
Bible Character Study Series

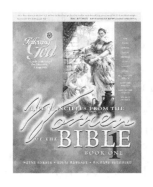

Life Principles from the Women of the Bible (Book One)

Characters include: Eve, Sarah, Miriam, Rahab, Deborah, Ruth, Hannah, Esther, The Virtuous Woman, Mary & Martha, Mary, the Mother of Jesus, and "The Bride of Christ."
ISBN 0-89957-302-9   224 pages

Life Principles from the Women of the Bible (Book Two)

Characters include: Hagar, Lot's Wife, Rebekah, Leah, Rachel, Abigail, Bathsheba, Jezebel, Elizabeth, The Woman at the Well, Women of the Gospels, and "The Submissive Wife."
ISBN 0-89957-308-8   224 pages

Life Principles from the New Testament Men of Faith

Characters include: John the Baptist, Peter, John, Thomas, James, Barnabas, Paul, Paul's Companions, Timothy, and "The Son of Man."
ISBN 0-89957-304-5   208 pages

Call for more information (800) 266-4977 or (423) 894-6060.

New Following God Release from AMG Publishers

Life Principles for Worship from the Tabernacle

ISBN 0-89957-299-5

This Bible study is designed in an interactive format, incorporating important scriptural points of interest and will help you understand all that God says to us through the components found in Israel's Tabernacle. Important historical and symbolic details will leap from the pages and into your heart. Inside the pages you'll also find the special helps sections you've come to rely on from the best-selling "Following God" series; Word Studies, Doctrinal Notes, Did You Know?, and Stop and Apply. Each help section will add to your understanding and ability to share these new-found truths with those you know and/or teach.

In the pages of this "Following God" study on the Tabernacle you'll learn to:

- ✓ Focus on the fence, the gate and the outer court with the bronze altar and bronze laver;
- ✓ Focus on the Holy Place with the golden lamp stand, the table of showbread, and the altar of incense;
- ✓ Move into the Holy of Holies through the veil, and look at the ark of the covenant with the golden jar of manna, Aaron's rod that budded, the tables of the covenant, the mercy seat and, ultimately, the cloud of glory.

Most importantly, you'll discover how God has provided a way for man to draw near to Him.

To order, call (800) 266-4977 or (423) 894-6060.

Leader's Guides for Following God™ books are available.
Watch for new Following God titles to be released soon!

New Following God Release from AMG Publishers

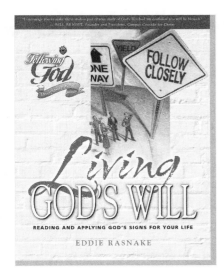

Living God's Will

ISBN 0-89957-309-6

How can I follow and identify the signs that lead to God's will? *Living God's Will* explores the answer to this all-important question in detail. It is Eddie Rasnake's deeply-held conviction that the road to God's will is well-marked with signposts to direct us. Each lesson in this twelve-week Bible study takes a look at a different signpost that reflects God's will. You will be challenged to recognize the signposts of God when you encounter them. But more importantly, you will be challenged to follow God's leading by following the direction of those signposts.

In the pages of this "Following God" study on finding and obeying God's will, you will find clear and practical advice for:

✓ Yielding your life to the Lord

✓ Recognizing God's will through Scripture, prayer and circumstances

✓ Seeking godly counsel

✓ Discovering how God's peace enters into the process of following His will

✓ Determining God's will in areas not specifically addressed in Scripture, such as choosing a wife/husband or career path.

Throughout your study you will also be enriched by the many interactive application sections that literally thousands have come to appreciate from the acclaimed **Following God** series.

To order, call (800) 266-4977 or (423) 894-6060.

Leader's Guidebooks for Following God™ books are now available. Watch for new Following God titles to be released soon!